MW01169838

MINDFULNESS FOR

WELL-BEING

Calm the Mind - Build Resilience

- Discover Optimal Health

An 8-Week Guide

DR. GLENDA RIVOALLAN

First and foremost, I dedicate this book to my wonderful husband, Jean, and son, Kaden, for your unwavering support. You have always been steadfast in encouraging me, even when I doubted myself.

Thanks from the bottom of my heart. I couldn't do it without you.

I would also like to thank my dearest friend, Fiona, for always supporting me and showering me with much love and compassion. You were naturally mindful, and although you sadly didn't get the chance to read this book, I know you are looking down on me with much pride.

I am eternally grateful to you, my beautiful angel.

Nanakorobi yaoki. (Fall seven times, stand up eight.)

—Japanese Proverb

CONTENTS

Foreword

I HAD THE GREAT honour of meeting Glenda when she came over my house for my two-day best-seller book retreat. At first, when she came in, she was very excited and had a lot of options on which way to go with her book. I then had some long conversations with Glenda and put her through some of my creativity exercises. Soon, this book you are about to read literally poured out of her!

I was in awe, hearing Glenda's powerful story and all of the lessons she has learned along the way.

The insights you will gain out of this book will stay with you forever, because they are timeless. Glenda understands how to live your best life, along with balancing a family and business.

One thing I would like for you to do as you read this book is to digest it slowly and savor each of the chapters. You will start to experience massive shifts in your consciousness and will also want to dive deeper into Glenda's *SOULGENIC* app, to deepen your understandings.

I hope you get what you want out of the book, as I did, and be sure to buy a copy for your friends and family members.

This masterpiece will be something you will cherish for a very long time.

I've read many books in my day, but this one will transform your life! It seriously gets my highest recommendation.

With Love,

AJ Mihrzad

Author of *The MIND BODY Solution: Train Your Brain for Permanent Weight Loss*

Founder of OnlineSupercoach.com

About This Book

THIS BOOK HAS BEEN written as a down-to-earth, practical introduction to using mindfulness for well-being. It is a hands-on guide, intended to help you reduce stress and improve your day-to-day well-being. Regardless of your age, financial status, or the so-called "baggage" you bring with you, you deserve to be happy. We *all* deserve happiness in our lives.

How to Use This Book

Mindfulness for Well-Being is designed as an eight-week guide that focuses on the four pillars of well-being which I consider to be fundamental for living a healthy, happy life. They include:

- **Fitness**
- **Nutrition**
- **Health**
- And that all-important **mind-body** connection

Through a different theme each week, we cover all four pillars of well-being and include one day for reflection on just how far you have come. We also include a day for rest, as sometimes we need to slow down in order to speed up (mindfulness teaches us this).

This easy-to-follow guide is suitable for all. We use a simple, guided structure designed to ensure it can be part of your daily routine.

With support and motivation throughout, each of the eight weeks has a theme for the entire week and a daily practice made up of two key elements: a daily activity and daily journal writing. Each week is structured as follows:

> ❖ **Day 1** starts with an introduction of the theme for the week with key insights and will include some activities to help you learn more about the underlying principles of mindfulness that I am keen to get across to you. These activities are designed to provide insight and are marked with a symbol:

> ❖ We introduce a mindfulness technique on **Day 2**, to give us the opportunity to practice it throughout the

week and give us that all-important **mind-body** connection (the fourth well-being pillar). These techniques are called a *mind-body connector* and are intended to help you bring mindfulness to life and again have their own symbol clearly marked:

❖ An activity each day (**Day 3-Day 5**) is included and centres around the theme of the week, to let you try out this way of living on each of the other three well-being pillars (**fitness, nutrition, and health**).

These are called *habit-breakers* and clearly marked with their own symbol. Habit-breakers are intended to help you to break free from limiting beliefs and actions. They are practices you can do in the midst of your everyday life and then grow them over a period of time.

❖ **Day 6** is set out as time to *reflect and recharge* and marked with its own symbol. It includes a summary of what we have covered:

❖ **Day 7** is our *rest* day (marked with a symbol) and time to *reward* our efforts:

Each day will ask you to record that you have completed the activity, that you have practiced the mind-body connector (whatever that may be), remind you how far you have come, and then will ask you to move on. It looks like this:

Complete   Y
Mind-body connector   Y
1/56
Move on

I WELCOME YOU TO JOIN ME ON THIS JOURNEY!

The Eight-Week Mindfulness for Well-Being Guide Overview

WEEK 1: THEME – WAKING UP

WEEK 2: THEME – COMING TO OUR SENSES

WEEK 3: THEME – MINDFULNESS OF THOUGHT

WEEK 4: THEME – EMBRACING DIFFICULTY

WEEK 5: THEME – THE JOY OF THE GREEN CICRLE

WEEK 6: THEME – FEEDING THE LOVE WOLF

WEEK 7: THEME – FINDING FLOW

WEEK 8: THEME – NOURISHING RESILIENCE

###

A FEW FURTHER NOTES before you read on:

I understand you may be really excited to get started and you may have a compulsion to jump the pages and get to the eight-week guide but... This is our first lesson in mindfulness. Learning to be patient and avoiding the need for instant fulfilment is a lesson in itself. If you are to get the most out of this book, it is important first of all to find out where I am coming from, review the evidence for mindfulness, including what it can potentially do for you and why I believe well-being is our greatest life-sustainer.

I am so excited to bring you this book and being able to demonstrate how mindfulness is incredibly relevant and appropriate to our modern lives. Many people think that mindfulness is an ancient practice that is not that relevant to our lives today and all about sitting cross-legged on a cushion in some mind-body studio or temple somewhere, meditating for hours on end.

However, I hope to show you that mindfulness does have its rightful place in the contemporary, often frantic world we now live in (more so than ever before) and specifically in helping us to train our brain for optimal well-being.

I hope that, through reading this book and trying all the activities, habit-breakers, and mind-body connectors included within its covers, you will begin to notice how mindfulness practice is not so much about sitting meditating but more about how we go about our lives, day to day, moment by moment, as our experiences unfold. The great thing about mindfulness is it can be seamlessly integrated into what you already do. I am not asking you to change what you do in your life. I am just asking you to do it in a more mindful way.

You may find some of the activities a little strange at first, and your mind may want to critique them, but aim to avoid this! You will learn in this book that your own mind can also be your own worst critic. I ask you to suspend over-thinking, judging, and analysing and to go with me on this important, potentially life-changing journey. It certainly worked for me…

The book is intended to not only act as a source of information but also as a journal: a place to record your practice and reflections. So please aim to write notes within the activity/journal sections (or in a personal journal, if you're reading an ebook edition), when you feel it's appropriate. Whatever springs to mind: a thought, feeling, or judgement, then please go ahead and document it. Research shows that writing things down helps us to better deal with stress, improve feelings of self-esteem, and better aid us in dealing with experiences.

So go ahead and write!

###

Chapter 1

Introduction

WHO AM I?

You may be wondering why this is even important in all of this, but... asking yourself *"who am I?"* is the first step to knowing how you got to here, regardless of where that may be, and asking this will help to give greater clarity to the future you strive for. Take some time out now to think about how you got to where you are today and how people and experiences have influenced you along the way, good or bad. Take it in...

Being in tune with how your life experiences have shaped who you have become and understanding why and how you think the way you do are crucial, if you are to challenge your thoughts and take positive action.

I have always been committed to my well-being, but it hasn't come to me on a plate.

I'm not one for blaming my childhood for my relatively low self-esteem, as I come from a very loving family, but my growing need for approval, need for achievement, and continual search for happiness developed as a result of early influence and experiences in my younger years, which left their mark on me.

I am the youngest sibling in a family of two girls. My father is English and my mother Scottish. Once both my parents set up home in Scotland, for all intents and purposes it was a traditional home, with my father being the breadwinner and my mother taking the role of housewife.

My mother had a fear of doing nothing and spent most of her life in an apron, cooking, cleaning, and then repeating, just to be sure. My father had an appeasing attitude towards my mother and would do anything to ensure he had my mum's back. Both my parents were extremely hard working, to the point where we lived counting down the days to our next holiday. I remember that clearly, and this work ethic passed down to me, with my parents' relentless standards influencing all aspects of my life: from school and sport to friends, to name a few. They weren't scared to tell you that you could do better next time, pick a better friend, or work harder at being better! It became the norm for me to work hard at all I did; to ensure my parents' were satisfied that I was going in the right direction. It was fully engrained in my brain that hard work = payoff, i.e., my mother and father's seal of approval.

My sister and I didn't spend a particularly great amount of time together. She was two years older than I, so I guess I must have come across as quite immature to her. She was a bit of a joker and took great delight in telling me I was adopted, which, to my knowledge, wasn't true...

So, if you are my parents, then please get in touch...!

As history has a habit of repeating itself, while I was growing up I spent endless hours trying to gain people's approval. I became more and more disappointed the more people rejected my advances or took advantage of my good nature. I guess I ultimately took refuge in sport.

This was something I really enjoyed, was really good at, and had a great sense of achievement from. At the same time, I also had a great ability to sell things—anything, really. People would say I could sell sand to the Arabs and snow to the Eskimos. Needless to say, as I entered my teenage years, my passion for all things sporty and my entrepreneurial spirit started to shine through, and I found great satisfaction in helping people with all things wellness related. At the age of sixteen, I was already out there, trying to stand out in the world with my branded car, marketing my own aerobics classes that I ran from a local church hall. My business career had officially begun, even if only in my spare time alongside my full-time studies.

In college, I was the class joker and charmingly called "G-spot" by my peers. I filled my college years with working on my physique as a means of becoming popular. It was something, again, I could control and something I was good at perfecting.

Perfecting is a good word, as it was during this time that I became more and more focused on achieving goals, even at the expense of my own well-being. It's something of a paradox that, in working so hard on being healthy, it had the reverse affect. I am sure some of you can relate to this: maybe working so hard on finding a partner that it actually doesn't happen; working too hard on gaining the perfect job that it never comes or can never live up to the promises. There is something about high expectations that, more often than not, sets you up for disappointment and a deep sense of unfulfilment and unhappiness—the opposite of what you seek!

A common occurrence in my career was I would drive so hard, with college work, study, exercise, friends, and anything else I could cram in, that I would end up with the common cold ("man flu," to some) every time I slowed down and prepared to take time out or go on holiday! It was a recognisable, vicious cycle that seemed to be on constant repeat: work, work, become unwell, rest, work harder, work even harder, become unwell, rest, repeat. Despite this lack of work/life balance, I ended up, through sheer drive and indomitable spirit, continuing my entrepreneurship journey in the wellness industry. I successfully founded multiple wellness-related businesses in a twenty-four-year period.

During this time, I navigated the enormous challenges placed on me as a result of being self-employed—e.g., fear of failure, risk and uncertainty—and I dealt with numerous challenges along the way. Don't get me wrong: there are many benefits to entrepreneurial life, but it can also be an extremely chaotic, restless, and intense existence. I coped with the demands admirably and on the surface had become very successful in my work life, until something smacked me in the face and halted me dead in my tracks, something to this day I didn't see coming and was not adequately prepared for.

Embracing Difficulty

My "hit you in the face" moment came shortly after I had two of the biggest career achievements in my life to date, whilst at the same time suffering in stealth silence due to an unhealthy work relationship. It is somewhat ironic that the hardest and unhappiest time of my life came after what appeared, on the surface to anyone looking, as a period of my life where I had "made it."

I had achieved a huge amount in my business life, but it didn't come without the down sides: my constant search for success and drive for perfection at the expense of relationships and non-work-related life-enriching experiences was becoming completely toxic. It crept up on me like a tiger stalking its prey in the dead of the night.

Then it happened: I had the thing we all dread. The big, all-encompassing meltdown.

I have suffered low points at various times in my life, self-managing bouts of tiredness, headaches, and mild depression along the way, but this episode was different. This was the top banana, the Big Ben of dark clouds that just wouldn't go away. I can't say why one unhealthy relationship was the thing that got me, but it was and it was big!

Unfortunately, this can happen to all of us, whether it's a death, divorce, lost job, or inability to lose weight—something that just sticks and pushes you on that dark, deep, downward spiral; one thing that tests every last bit of resilience you have. For me, this was it.

The long and short of it is that I crashed and burned and drove off the cliff of healthiness. Looking back now, it is quite ironic that the drive and hard work that had served me so well now became the very thing that was my undoing, in dealing with difficulty. The years of hard work had left their mark on me, and I just didn't have the vigour, energy, or resilience to embrace the issues engulfing me. The joy of work faded to a dull, persistent ache.

I proceeded to spend a few months in fight-or-flight mode, and the situation just got worse. Being in a highly stressful environment, especially one that is prolonged, erodes the very resources you have to tackle things head-on. The only way I can describe this is I was operating with tunnel vision. I had become so stressed that I felt powerless to act and just couldn't see options open to me. I felt completely overwhelmed: overpowered by both the circumstances and the resulting feelings. What ensued was a mental numbness. I retreated inward, becoming less responsive to others. I had a deep desire to be alone and a noticeable inability to focus. I became more and more indecisive the further down the road I went.

When the body feels under attack, its aim is to survive, and so there is no space left for the very things that can maintain your resolve. The result was that my energy levels were drained, so my fitness suffered. My love for eating evaporated so my nutrition suffered. Physical signs, such as increased headaches, muscle fatigue, weeping, and ringing ears, highlighted in Technicolour how my health was suffering. I lost that all-important mind-body connection, too, which manifested itself in my snapping under pressure, being reactive in my decision-making rather than proactive, and generally being very withdrawn.

Quite frankly, I felt like a huge fraud. Here I was, selling well-being to the masses, but I was the unhealthiest and most unfulfilled I had ever been at any time of my life.

What materialised was months of sadness, feelings of worthlessness, and ultimately a dark and scary depression. The problem with these emotions is they play havoc on your relationships. When I was depressed, I cut myself off from people, even family, the result being I got even more depressed. It's like an iPod on repeat: the very behaviour that caused me to get depressed played out on a repetitive loop, causing me to get even more depressed – I felt like a hamster on a wheel.

A Timely Discovery

Right in the middle of this difficult situation, I embarked on an eight-week mindfulness course after a chance meeting at a barbeque, where I met Dr. Alessio Agostinis, a very cool guy who just happened to be a mindfulness practitioner. This course quite literally changed my life forever.

Little did I know at the time that everything I was learning with Alessio would become so critical in helping me pull myself out of this pit of despair. It was quite simply remarkable and surprisingly easy to fit into my life. I now have philosophical moments where I get in touch with my spirituality, as I honestly feel someone or something with a higher purpose put the course right in my path when I most needed it. I guess it often happens this way, if you believe life has a greater meaning. For me, this was a precious gift.

The foundation of mindfulness is a practice that offers us the ability to wake up and become present in our everyday lives. It helps us to awaken, to develop the wisdom life brings when we experience it for all that it is, and it teaches us to respond rather than habitually react to people and external events.

I look back on that time and wonder where I would be now, if I hadn't found the techniques of mindfulness at that time. It actually scares me to think about what may have happened if I hadn't experienced the incredible benefits of this practice. In undertaking the mindfulness course, the tools, techniques, and tips I discovered (which I will teach you throughout this book) taught me to stay curious, open, and interested.

Once I got comfortable in the mud, things started to get more interesting, as ideas and possibilities became clearer to me the more self-aware I became. I began to challenge my own thoughts and limiting beliefs, and it was quite liberating to wake up to the notion of me being able to accept that the notion of thoughts being the only truth or narrative is something I have control over accepting or not.

Rather than feeling stuck and helpless, I took control of my own happiness. I realised I couldn't change things that had happened to me in the past, no matter how long and how hard I tried to change them. I could choose to continue to be angry, sad, and stressed, or I could choose to do something about it.

I had to wake up to the fact that the past and future are not concrete things, and the only tangible thing is what I can do in the here and now in the present. I decided to stop putting power in the hands of others by focusing on what they need to change, and I embraced my own self, instead. What transpired over the coming months was I became much more aware of myself and began to see myself as I really am. I became more content with enjoying the present and became so much happier as a result.

But, for me, the single most valuable insight I gained from mindfulness training was a renewed sense of compassion for both myself and others. Mindfulness made such a difference in my life that I moved on to study mindfulness and its role in developing resilience in entrepreneurs at the doctorate level.

My five years of research have shown me that mindfulness improves your resilience. It gives you the tools to fall down seven times but get back up eight!

I have since discovered that my intense habitual need for achievement and acceptance had lost its pull on me. When something or someone in your life is not aligned to your way of thinking, then it has potential for great toxicity and more often than not is going to result in tears (metaphorically speaking). I decided after much soul-searching that I could not continue to forfeit my happiness for status or title.

I will stop here for a second... I speak to so many people who stay in a job, marriage, or friendship despite being intensely unhappy. But I ask you this: how many people stay doing something or avoid doing something because they feel safe in their comfort zone? How many of those people will tell you as much as you care to listen to that they are miserable, unhappy, demotivated, and often all three? Well, I now know, when you cut ties with people or things that are toxic to you, in breaking free from something that is limiting your own growth, you will become much happier as a result. It's true what Simon Sinek, a well-known guru in leadership, says: the real magic happens outside of the "circle of comfort".

I am not going to say that really big decisions don't come without trepidation and anxiety; also, they don't always work out as they should. In my case, mindfulness helped me to better avoid excessive rumination and worry about the future, all the "what ifs?" I arrived at a place where I could put the unpleasantness of the past behind me, where I was at peace with how I wanted it to end and that I could control the outcome.

Mindfulness helped me manage the situation, and I have no doubt it further developed my resilience to tackle the consequences of my decision. I was better able to handle my emotions, make sense of the experience without resorting to overthinking and negativity, and maintain positive behaviours and actions to help me find a way to climb out of what was a very dark and dreary place. There was no doubt I was more at peace with the situation and a whole lot happier, knowing I had decided to cut ties with a relationship that was clearly causing me harm and upset.

The unexpected learning that this unsavoury depressive episode served me was that I began to realize I had used my success as armour to cover the chaos inside me. I had created a fabrication: I was just a front, and behind the front, no one was home. I began to realize that being an entrepreneur was a fantastic antidote to dysfunctional aspects of my life—it was a form of escapism.

Mindfulness awakened my thinking to my own well-being and the importance of investing in my own well-being as a means of maintaining my resilience to enable me to face challenges. Subsequently, by focusing in on my fitness, my nutrition, my health, and my mind-body connection, I remerged out of the darkness.

It was from finding the power of mindfulness and its impact on my well-being that I decided to develop a well-being app, which includes mindfulness at its core.

Now I have written this book with the hope of helping others who need to let go or start something new. I am happier than I have ever been. I am not saying I am completely cured of all that hurts my head, the need to achieve, and the need to do everything at 100 miles per hour, but I am getting better at understanding the need to sometimes slowdown in order to speed up.

Chapter 2

Why Well-Being?

THERE IS ONE thing we all have in common: we need to wake up and put well-being at the heart of our personal life, work life, and everything else we care to partake in.

I put this to you: there are no rich people in the graveyard, there are no people out there who can give their best to their relationships if they are so stressed they can't think straight, and there is no one out there who will get the best from their body, if they pollute it with smoke, alcohol, and every other concoction known to man.

I know it's common sense, but if we are not healthy then what do we have? If we can't look after our own well-being, then how can we look after our partners, our children, our businesses, and so on? It never fails to amaze me the amount of people who don't think twice about spending 100 pounds on a night out but won't spend 60 pounds a month or 1.94 a day on a health club membership. We will happily pay more for a cup of coffee per day!

For the sake of our relationships, our work, and our happiness, this mindset needs to shift. If we don't tackle the tide of stress that is about to engulf us and then develop strategies for coping, we are sitting on an even bigger detonator than the small grenades that go off in our heads currently, draining our resilience as we live our day-to-day lives!

The Stress Epidemic

We are all stressed out.... Yes, all of us.... Well, most of us... Me included... And for me, that's too many.

It seems hard to believe that despite those of "us'" in developed countries looking pretty lucky on the surface (free of hunger, disease, and war), we complain of more and more stress. Despite our fantastic triumphs, including free speech, successful space exploration, and technological advancements to the point where artificial intelligence is just around the corner, we are nonetheless heading towards meltdown. In our attempts to explore all things interesting and external to us, we have failed to explore ourselves and what is lurking internally in our own being.

We just keep trying to compete and achieve with absolutely no understanding as to why. One could say we have focused on goals at the expense of values. But at what cost? "Stress" has been dubbed the "Health Epidemic of the 21st Century" by the World Health Organization and is estimated to cost UK businesses up to £1 billion a year on lost productivity. But, more than work, what impact is prolonged stress and the chaos inside our heads having on our ability to have fulfilled relationships both with ourselves and others? We now know that when a person is in a state of constant stress, many weird and not-so-wonderful things happen to their physiology, including increased rates of heart attack, hypertension, obesity, cancer, addiction, anxiety, depression, feelings of isolation, and other disorders, to name a few.

But here is the really interesting thing about stress: it is fundamentally not necessarily manifested by a true reality; rather, and more importantly, by the person's perception of that reality. That's why we know some people appear to cope with high levels of demands placed upon them but others crumble at the first sign of a challenge. The good news is we can do a lot to reframe our thinking and deal with our perceptions of stress, negating its potential for negative impact.

So why does stress have such a grip on us?

The Evolution of our Brains

Our brains were never built to cope with the demands placed upon us in the fast-paced, constantly changing world we now live in. Things were not so complex when we came into the world. There was not as great a need for multi-tasking and doing everything at a relentless pace. We were more content with what we had. Essentially, our primitive brain was built to look out for danger and protect our young at all costs. Life has moved on somewhat since those days. Yes, we need to ensure we have enough get up and go and built-in warning mechanisms so, if we go to cross the road and a bus appears, we can avoid getting run over.

However, this useful brain function can make us feel more stressed than is necessary, if we are on constant alert looking out for danger. Understanding how your brain became so vigilant, wary, and so easily hijacked by alarm is the first step toward gaining more control over the brain's medieval wiring.

By bringing mindful awareness to how your brain reacts to feeling threatened, you can stimulate and therefore build up the neural pathways of a mind-set that is calmer, wiser, and stronger. A mind that sees real threats more clearly, acts more effectively in dealing with them, and is less rattled or distracted by exaggerated worries and unhelpful thoughts.

Negativity Bias

The big problem is that our brain's construction hasn't changed and still performs this fight-or-flight function, even though we rarely need this function to come to our rescue. Neuro-psychologists call this the *negativity bias,* where we accept negative thoughts and feelings much more readily than positive ones; we are designed to see the imperfections in a situation, the potential threats to our well-being. Specifically, we tend to overestimate threats, underestimate opportunities, and underrate our in-built resources and coping mechanisms for tackling challenges that present themselves to us.

Our brains developed the way they did to ensure the human race survives, not to make us happy and content! It's hard to relax and enjoy yourself when your "danger" radar is fully turned up. Imagine trying to enjoy yourself in your job if you feel someone there wants to sabotage your work and push you out! It doesn't feel good...

What's more, when we notice the negative, it immediately gets stored in our memory, whereas any positive experiences need to be held in awareness for a dozen or more seconds to transfer from short-term memory to long-term storage. Neuropsychologist Rick Hanson, Ph.D. and author of *Hardwiring Happiness* argues that our brains are like Velcro for negative experiences and like Teflon for positive ones with potentially disastrous consequences for our contentment, confidence and resulting happiness.

There are many ways in which this negativity bias manifests itself in playing havoc on our well-being too. Here are some examples:

> ➢ We remember people being disrespectful to us more than we remember them expressing approval.
> ➢ We find that negative experiences tend to be more memorable than positive ones.
> ➢ We often find it hard to develop new habits as we fixate on past failings and inadequacies.
> ➢ We often habitually pull away from things that are difficult, e.g., building new health habits.
> ➢ We struggle to make change and we put it into the "I will do it tomorrow" category, as it is safer to stay in your comfort zone of what you know and do.

So we need to work against this to avoid our in-built hard-wired negativity bias that can create chaos with our thoughts and feelings. Developing mindfulness of both the inner workings of your brain and the outer mechanisms of needless fear, which can often result in us feeling stuck, staying with the status quo, or avoiding tackling our problems altogether, is an important skill to master.

In turning our attention to as many positive, pleasant and memorable experiences as bad ones, we are beginning to develop a more balanced and objective appraisal of our situation. We are not looking at our life through rose-tinted spectacles. Far from it. We are simply enabling ourselves to see ourselves as we really are!

Living With the Enemy

I now appreciate more than ever what is meant when someone says you are "your own worst enemy." For me, whether you are wanting to get fit, lose weight, or improve your relationship with food, the single most important thing that gets in your way is **YOURSELF**.

It's only since practicing mindfulness that I fully realized we are the sabotagers of our own happiness. I often joke with my friends that we are often living with the enemy, that voice in our head that all-too-often is overly critical of what we want to do, are about to do, or have done in the past. I refer to my inner critic as Clive. Quite frankly, Clive can be a real pain in my ass, getting in the way and trying to undo all the good work I do. My friend, an online coach, refers to hers as her evil twin!

You don't get Olympic athletes allowing Clive or their evil twin a space in their head, especially rent-free! They don't turn up to represent their countries in their sport thinking they don't deserve to be there. They don't focus on all their deficiencies, and they aren't thinking they will be sent packing without a medal.

To get on and achieve what you set out to achieve involves a boundless reserve of self-confidence. If we brought to our well-being journey the same mindset elite athletes bring to their sport, we would have a much stronger chance of success. The reality is that harboring secret demons such as fear of failure, lack of belief, and a search for perfection is all too common and even more so in women. In particular, women struggle through moments of near-debilitating anxiety and despair, times when it seems that everything might fall apart.

The science tells us that women are more judgmental than their male counterparts. Women are much more highly self-critical about their looks, their mistakes, their relationships, their work success, etc., than men. You may have heard that a man will apply for a job if they tick sixty percent of the job description, while a woman will not apply if they can't tick ninety-five percent of the same specification.

Many women have an addiction to perfection that ultimately impacts their self-confidence. Women struggle to ignore the inner voice of negative self-talk that repeatedly seeks to undermine their work. You don't hear men saying, "I feel so guilty spending all that time away from the kids, playing golf and tennis on the weekend." In talking about their latest success, you don't hear them say, "I was just lucky!" And you definitely don't hear them say, "My bum looks massive in this."

Prolonged self-doubt can result in any of us being vulnerable to mental health issues. A lack of recognition or self-awareness of this state of mind may lead us to march on regardless, engaging with unhealthy automatic behavioral patterns, which can lead to burnout or soul sickness as a result of permanent stress. For the sake of our health and our happiness, we need to tackle this inner critic head-on and challenge the very thoughts that often give us a distorted view of our own reality.

In Search of Happiness

Happiness—or at least my *perception* of it—has been something I always felt I had to chase. It has felt like a lifelong expedition of discovery. Rather than see happiness as just a by-product of the activities I find enjoyable, I would go after it with appetite, striving way too hard to do things I thought would make me happy.

According to Zhuang Zhou, an influential Chinese philosopher, "Happiness is the absence of striving for happiness." If that's the case, I wonder how many of my friends and colleagues are genuinely happy. I mean, just like me, many of us wake up each morning and organise our days around what will make us happy (or, at least, what we *think* will make us happy).

We cram in to our lives as much as possible, because we think socialising will make us happy. We go out even when we can't be bothered, faking enjoyment, because staying home would simply be a complete waste of time and frowned upon. We even resort to spending our nights hoping someone we like gives us the attention we crave, whether that's a Facebook message, a phone call, or a ping from WhatsApp. Well, if you're the kind of person who puts a lot of time and effort into being happy, the best thing you could do for yourself might be not trying at all because, in pursuing happiness, it might be the very thing that's holding you back.

Being happy and having a positive outlook are important for a healthy mind. But when you force yourself to be overly optimistic, you may inadvertently negatively impact your spirit. You will more than likely enter a state of denial, repressing emotions that you should try to work through instead and put them into the "I will tackle these later" box.

The paradox is, before we can overcome sadness, we need to experience it. The way forward beyond sadness is not to avoid it but to tackle it. Although you might be feeling down and think that doing "happy things" will pull you out of it, you'll probably just conceal your unhappiness. Granted, you may temporarily forget about your problems. But suppressing your feelings will guarantee you never truly overcome challenges that present themselves. You're just putting them off.

Mindfulness taught me that we need to *stop striving for happiness.* We need to stop thinking of it as something to be worked on. Happiness is something that will take over when it's real, but it should not be hunted. My friend, a dating coach, likened it to finding love in that, when you try too hard to find it, you'll only end up putting everyone else's needs before your own. You also lose perspective and blind yourself to all the possibilities. The resulting tunnel vision inevitably results in you not find the very thing you seek.

In order to be truly happy, we need to take a step back and allow ourselves to be truly happy. The mindfulness tools I will put to you throughout this book will hopefully aid you in developing an acceptance of where you are in the here and now. Being accepting of where you are and following the "less is more" principle are the first steps to becoming less stressed and hopefully happier and more fulfilled as a result.

Constant Connection

With the constant evolution of technology, we now live in a world with persistent connectivity. This has resulted in many of us rarely switching off and having time out; we are constantly connected. The growth of platforms such as Facebook, Instagram, and Twitter has resulted in many people having a fear of missing out. This relates to the idea of a feeling of uneasiness that a person might get from the sense they are missing out on social experiences that other people might be having. The perception that other people are having more fulfilling life experiences than they, themselves, are has resulted in many people having stronger feelings of low self-esteem and self-worth as a result of negative views of their own self-image.

Erving Goffman, in the book *The Presentation of Self in Everyday Life,* says people can change the way they act or want to appear in different scenarios. Goffman's theory is there are two personas when it comes to the persistent connectivity of the Internet: the "I" persona and the "me" persona. The "I" is always present in some way, but it is usually backstage, behind the mask out front. The mask shows the "me" persona and is influenced by the persona behind it. The "me" persona shows how the person *wants* to be seen and may be seen as the one engaging in online activities.

Aside from the obvious challenges, the notion of "keeping up with the Joneses" using the me persona places upon us, research is showing us that being constantly connected is playing havoc with our relationships and our stress levels, as a result of becoming overwhelmed by information overload. Our "always on" attitude leads to a constant state of ambient anxiety, which is damaging psychologically. Mindfulness will teach us about the importance of switching off and having time for peace and serenity in our lives.

Multi-tasking

There is no doubt the pace by which we live our lives is faster than ever before: travel is faster, food is faster, communication is faster; we live in a world where technological advancement has resulted in everything being faster. We receive hundreds of emails, endless texts, WhatsApp notifications, and so on per day instead of one or two letters every now and again. It's easy to get caught up in the rat race that life has become, maintaining a diary bursting at the seams, moving from one activity to another without as much as pausing for thought, or even juggling multiple things at once as we rush through our day. The problem with multi-tasking and rushing is they can become habitual, so even when we don't need to do something quickly or complete multiple things at once, we still do (People still eat at their desk even when they're not in a rush).

Doing everything quickly and juggling multiple demands at once has quite a bad effect on us over the long term:

> ➤ It activates the fight-or-flight response, causing us to be on red alert for danger. This can result in overthinking, excessive rumination, and worry.

> ➤ It activates the stress-response system, releasing unhelpful chemicals into our bloodstream. These hormones weaken your immune system, making you prone to illness. They can also lower your mood.
> ➤ It gives us less time to think clearly and make good decisions.
> ➤ It can result in a feeling of emptiness when not in "doing" mode.

It's safe to say it's time to *slow down in order to speed up.* We cannot possibly be productive if we live on next to no sleep, work all day, don't stop for breaks, and continue way into the night. The one thing about being human is exactly that—that we are human! And humans need rest. Without it, we cannot possibly thrive. It is like buying a plant and then depriving it of light or water.

Four Pillars of Well-being

I strongly believe that to discover true well-being involves a 360-degree approach to health, a rounded holistic strategy that encompasses not only fitness but also nutrition, health, and that all-important mind-body connection.

This ethos runs through everything I recommend and it is why my fitness club has services on all four pillars. The well-being app I have developed is built around these four pillars, too.

You cannot discover true well-being if you only do fitness but don't care about what you eat, or if you eat well but never get sweaty, or if you eat and exercise but never get a good night's sleep. The toughest of buildings always have four corners, to give strength to their foundation. It's no different with your well-being, the four pillars gives us strength. There is never a truer saying that a healthy body is a healthy mind.

We all want the mindset that allows us to be at peace whilst driving to work, or the mindset that allows us to think and act responsively rather than reactively, when engaging in relationships. Or the mindset that helps us to stop being stuck in past experiences or failings or worrying about too far ahead in the future. The truth is attaining such a state of mind is one of our greatest challenges, but it can be within your grasp.

This is what *Mindfulness for Well-being* brings. Improvements in mindfulness will help you with improvements in well-being and vice versa. They are intrinsic to each other.

This book gives you an integrated well-being journey and will provide you tools, techniques, and tips throughout the eight-week guide in the following ways, which will allow you to:

- ✓ Become aware of the positive and nurturing opportunities that are available to you on all four pillars of health by respecting your own inner wisdom.
- ✓ Use all your senses in making choices that are both satisfying to you and nourishing to your body.
- ✓ Acknowledge responses to things (likes, dislikes) without judgment.
- ✓ Become aware of cues to guide your decisions to begin adopting healthier habits.
- ✓ Acknowledge there is no right or wrong way to being healthier, but varying degrees of awareness surrounding the experience.
- ✓ Accept that your well-being experiences are unique, that you are an individual who, by choice, directs their attention to well-being on a moment-by-moment basis.
- ✓ Become more focused on how the mind serves the body and how the body serves the mind.

✓ Become more aware of how the mind-body connection can improve your resilience and, ultimately, your well-being.

Chapter 3

Mindfulness For Well-Being

SO WHAT EXACTLY IS mindfulness?

Mindfulness came about as a result of the unusual fusion of Eastern philosophy and practice combined with modern psychological principles. Mindfulness is not about zoning out or withdrawing from the world. You don't need to retreat to a Buddhist temple or commit to becoming a Buddhist monk in order to tap into the benefits of a regular practice. It's about developing your awareness in your everyday life so that stress-free thinking replaces habitual thought processes that can often hold you back.

Jon Kabat-Zinn, probably the most famous mindfulness teacher and the man who created the mindfulness-based stress-reduction course, sees it as an "***awareness*** that emerges through paying ***attention*** on purpose, in the ***present*** moment, and ***non-judgmentally*** to the unfolding of ***experience*** as it happens." Mindfulness is about focusing your attention on the present moment whilst calmly acknowledging your feelings, thoughts, bodily sensations, and overall experience.

Simply put, mindfulness means knowing directly what is going on inside and outside ourselves, as it happens. It's easy to stop noticing the world around us. It's also easy to lose touch with the ways our bodies are feeling and end up living "in our heads"—caught up in thinking without stopping to notice how those thoughts are driving our emotions and behaviour.

An important part of mindfulness is reconnecting with our bodies and the sensations they experience. This means waking up to the sights, sounds, smells, and tastes of the present moment. That might be something as simple as noticing the sound of the waves as we walk along the beach. It's about allowing ourselves to see the present moment clearly. When we do that, it can positively change the way we see ourselves and our lives.

Just like learning any new skill, mindfulness takes practice, but when it becomes a key part of your everyday life, it has been proven to be helpful in a variety of ways. Mindfulness practice has been proven to lower blood pressure, reduce chronic pain, improve sleep, reduce the harmful stress hormone cortisol, and reduce age-related deterioration of aspects of the brain. The long and short of it is MINDFULNESS IMPROVES YOUR WELL-BEING.

The Science of Sitting

Until recently, positing that hours of sitting meditation could alter the pathology of the brain would have been at odds with established beliefs. Up until the 1990s, scientific convention held that after a critical period of "plasticity" early in life, the brain's basic architecture is set in stone, essentially fixing our neural wiring in place for life. This limited belief about our control over whether or not we could make our brain stronger or more inclined to focus on positive emotions is, in part, the reason why researchers at the time reinforced trait theories that we were either born resilient or not.

Advances in MRIs and other neuroimaging technologies, have led to a revolution in how we think about the capacity of our brains. We now understand that our neural pathways continue to develop throughout our lifetime.

The knowledge that the architecture of our brains is not static, that it can change, and this notion of "neuroplasticity" have resulted in a surge in mindfulness research. This emerging knowledge changed the way researchers assess mindfulness as a holistic practice and as a means of improving psychological well-being. Research by Lowel and Singer on neuroplasticity confirms, "Neurons that fire together, wire together." With training, the neural pathways that regulate our emotions, thoughts, and reactions can be rewired. "The mind can change the brain, and a changed brain can then change the mind" (Hanson, 2013).

Clarity in a World of Calamity

Mindfulness is concerned with cultivating the quality of being awake, present, and accepting of this moment's experience—which has a transforming potential on how we are with ourselves, how we are with others, and how we are with stressful, difficult, and challenging situations. I truly believe that mindfulness has the potential to give you clarity in a world that is prone to calamity. Whether you see yourself as chilled out or highly strung, we are all at risk of stress as a result of the pace at which we lead our lives.

More and more research on mindfulness (including my own) has shown that improvements in mindfulness help to improve resilience and well-being by reducing the impact of stress.

Stressful things happen: we might be having a relationship difficulty or struggling to lose weight or feeling low about our exercise regime or lack of and so on. That's our genuine, first hand experience, and we can't do very much about it. However, we often cause ourselves extra, unnecessary stress by reacting to that experience with attaching judgements and labels to various thoughts and feelings.

For instance, let's say you are struggling to get fit. You might have such thoughts as, "I'll never manage to get control of my exercise," or "Why did I agree to do this training programme in the first place?" accompanied by feelings of resentment, inadequacy, and anxiety. And adding judgments about others such as, "Why is he getting me to do such a stupid exercise?" or the self "I'm useless at this". These kinds of reactions often tend to snowball or multiply—one thought to many more thoughts, leading to more feelings, leading to more judgments. They're also obsessional, trapping us in the problem that we're trying to solve. Before we know it, we're trapped in a psychic prison of unhappiness!

Mindfulness helps to avoid tunnel vision as a result of stress and allows us to open up our minds to possibility. Developing mindfulness helps us become more resilient in that it helps us acquire the knowledge, abilities, and skills to face the uncertain future with a positive attitude, with creativity and optimism, and by relying on our own resources.

Mindfulness has helped me to develop the necessary coping skills to tackle life with optimism, hope, and clarity. I now put these to you.

Chapter 4

The Eight-Week Mindfulness for Well-Being Guide

HOW EXCITING THAT YOU are now at the start of a mindfulness journey that may just help you to move towards greater well-being and the life you want and deserve!

This eight-week guide has been developed to bring your well-being into sharp focus and has been developed from the reading and learning I have done through studying for my doctorate in mindfulness, my twenty-four years of experience in the wellness industry, and from working closely with two highly experienced practitioners in the teaching of mindfulness utilising mindfulness-based therapies.

In the next few weeks (fifty-six days, to be exact), we will work together to discover the benefits of this incredible practice. You will be encouraged through the activities to begin to introduce mindfulness in your everyday life and continue long after the eight weeks end, using my Soulgenic well-being app. I invite you to go on this journey with an open mind and to do what you can in whatever way works for you.

The activities given amounts to around forty-five minutes per day as a mixture of both formal (thirty minutes) and more informal activities, applying skills into things you do every day (fifteen minutes). So do the daily activities where possible.

If you view mindfulness as *gym* for the mind and a *tonic* for life's difficulties, then the quantity and type of practice are important. In the following pages, you will find all that you need to know or learn in order to begin practicing mindfulness.

Good luck and enjoy!

Healthy regards,

Glenda

The time is now—it's time to make the change!

Pre-Course Goal Setting

Take time to consider what you want to achieve in terms of your well-being. After careful consideration and reflection, complete the sections below:

By the end of the 8 weeks, I want to achieve:

Fitness: _____

_____

_____

_____

Nutrition: _____

_____

_____

_____

Health: _____

_____

_____

_____

MindBody: _____

_____

_____

In the box below, write a pledge to yourself as a source of inspiration and as a reminder of what you want to achieve:

GLENDA RIVOALLAN

When I complete this eight weeks, my reward will be (Write in the space below):

_____
_____
_____
_____
_____
_____
_____
_____
_____
_____
_____

It Starts Here: WEEK 1 THEME - WAKING UP

Day 1 – Insight

Day 2 - Mind-body connector (body scan)

Day 3 – Fitness habit-breaker (one small thing)

Day 4 – Nutrition habit-breaker (one small thing)

Day 5 – Health habit-breaker (one small thing)

Day 6 - Reflect & Recharge

Day 7 – Rest & reward

Day 1 Insight:

"Collect moments, not things"

—April Peerless

We tend to go about our daily lives spending a vast amount of time operating on "autopilot." You may have driven or walked somewhere—arriving at your destination and on reflection noticed that you have no real recollection as to how you got there.

We eat a meal and have no recollection of how it tasted. We go to an exercise class and do not savour the good work we have done. We read a page of this book and can't remember the key points.

We often miss the small details before we "come round" and recognize what has happened. This is because we are quite able to piece together numerous habitual activities and complete them as one in a largely automatic fashion.

Thanks to the human brain, we are able to perform without the need for much conscious thought. The downside of this innate ability is we end up staying on automatic pilot, not noticing anything around us. With mindfulness, we aim to develop a greater awareness of the present.

Mindfulness means deliberately acknowledging and becoming more aware of our thoughts, feelings, and physical responses. In essence, the practice is first and foremost about waking up and noticing your experience as it unfolds. The aim this week is to become more aware of primary experiences, i.e., sensory information (primary experiences) such as sound, touch, smell, breathing, etc., as opposed to secondary experiences, i.e., thoughts and overthinking, which are often like grenades going off in your head—they can be very unhelpful and negative.

Mindfulness helps us deal with stressful situations by continually helping us to come back to our primary experience. When we are not very aware, running on autopilot, often overthinking and not being in tune with what we are doing, things happen to us, and we react in habitual ways—like quickly moving into fight-or-flight mode, becoming defensive and adopting a negative mind-set.

When we are more aware, we develop greater knowledge of what is happening and begin to see ourselves and things as they really are. We can come to recognize prompts that trigger unhelpful thoughts and behaviour and we become aware of thoughts and feelings that are gradually building up.

This week is all about waking up and noticing things that, more often than not, we take for granted.

Habit-breaker Exercise

Every week, we're going to introduce one habit-breaker you can easily incorporate into your everyday life to promote mindfulness and reduce stress. This week we want to encourage you to do **one small thing** that takes very little time but can have impactful effects.

Doing one small thing on its own won't produce very big results, but doing it a number of times a day can make a huge difference. As an example, just like if you were to enrol for a triathlon and start training in the gym, unless you start transferring that preparation outside into the real environment, by swimming, cycling and running it will be difficult if not impossible to complete it with any success.

Habit-breakers will help you to do exactly that: they will help you to break the cycle of working in the default position using "automatic" pilots, making you more aware, helping you to transfer mindfulness techniques into everyday life and therefore create new habits. These habit-breakers are gym exercises for the mind that develop mindfulness over time.

This week's habit-breaker is to bring mindful attention to something you do *every day,* such as having a shower or bath, cleaning your teeth, walking up and/or down stairs, eating a meal, drinking a cup of water.

This habit-breaker won't take any extra time out of your day, because you do these things anyway so it's an easy place to start.

Select one normal daily task from the list above and stay with anything sensory about that experience: taste, smell, sound, movement—and the flow of change of that sensory input.

Whatever you chose, just aim to do it mindfully, which simply means paying attention to whatever you are doing moment by moment.

It means guiding your mind back to what you're doing whenever it strays off onto something else, which it probably will do numerous times even when drinking a glass of water, for example. This is the purpose of the practice: to notice primary experiences and, if you go off on little thoughts or images appear (secondary experiences with grenades going off in your head), keep coming back to primary (the here and now) and stay connected to the experience.

Day 1 Activity: One small thing

Daily task:

_____

_____

Today's observations:

_____

_____

_____

_____

Complete Y

1/56

Move on

Day 2: Mind-Body Connector

Each week, we will ask you to practice a mind-body connector (a mindfulness technique designed to develop the mind-body connection). This week's mind-body connector is **the body scan.** Many people like to do this lying down, although you can also do it sitting up. This simple body scan is a fantastic way to start the day. Instead of propelling yourself straight into your busy day, a more mindful start will help you feel better prepared to deal with the stressors that arrive at work and at home.

Whether you choose to lie down or sit up, find a comfortable position that you feel best supports a relaxed state of mind. Your arms can either be down at your sides, the palms facing upwards, or you can rest your hands lightly on the stomach, with the palms facing downwards.

Now close your eyes and breathe in a natural way. Bring your attention to your breathing: both to your in-breath, and to your out-breath following it throughout. Continue to do this until you feel fully relaxed.

Now bring your attention to the top of your head and begin to notice any sensations you feel. It might be a body sensation such as tingling or your body temperature, hot or cold. Don't worry what they are. The important thing is to be aware of these feelings.

Now move your attention down to your face, jaw, neck, and shoulders, maintaining awareness of bodily sensations of each body part. Notice your arms and hands, stomach and back. Then bring your attention to your pelvis, buttocks, your thighs, lower legs, and feet. As you progress from one body part to another, become aware of any tensions in any body part.

Finally, take one last deep breath. Embrace the sensation and simply acknowledge your intention to bring this peace of mind to everything you do as you progress through the day.

Day 2 Activity: Body scan

Today's observations:

_____

_____

_____

_____

_____

_____

_____

Complete Y
2/56
Move on

NOW AIM TO PRACTICE THE BODY SCAN EVERY MORNING FOR THE REST OF THE WEEK, ALONGSIDE YOUR DAILY ACTIVITY.

Day 3 Fitness Habit-breaker

Today we are going to practice what you learned at the start of the week by doing **one small thing** with a *focus on fitness*. The key objective in this exercise is to ensure whatever fitness exercise you chose, e.g., stretching, jogging, squats, you try to do it mindfully using the same technique outlined in Day 1. Pay attention to how the exercise feels. Note any changes in your breathing, what muscle groups you sense, etc. Force your senses to wake up! Select an exercise and record it below.

Day 3 Activity: Fitness – one small thing

Exercise:

_____

_____

Today's observations:

_____

_____

_____

_____

_____

Day 4 Nutrition Habit-breaker

Today we are going to practice what you learned at the start of the week by doing **one small thing** with a *focus on nutrition.* The key objective in this exercise is to ensure that whatever piece of food you choose, e.g., one piece of chocolate, one strawberry, one grape, that you eat it mindfully using the same technique outlined in Day 1.

Pay attention to every sound, the feel of it in your hand, the colour, and pay close attention to the taste when you move it around your mouth.

Force your senses to wake up! Select a food choice and record it below.

Day 4 Activity: Nutrition – one small thing

Food Choice:

_____

_____

Today's observations:

_____

_____

_____

_____

_____

_____

_____

Complete Y
+Body scan Y/N
4/56
Move on

Day 5 Health Habit-breaker

Today we are going to practice doing **one small thing** with a *focus on health*. This activity is focused on getting you to wake up to your current health status. Even by becoming more aware of your health status and noticing when things impact your health, you are then more likely to do one small thing to make a positive difference.

Answer the questions below after reflecting on the question posed. Then pledge to do one small thing to improve your health.

Day 5 Activity: Health – one small thing

Ask yourself:

Do you suffer stress on a regular basis? Y/N

Do you eat a healthy balanced diet? Y/N

Do you take regular exercise? Y/N

Do you feel a mind-body connection? Y/N

Is there anything else hindering your health? Y/N

Write down the number-one thing hindering your health

_____

_____

_____

What one small thing can you commit to doing to improve how this impacts your health?

_____

_____

_____

Complete Y
+Body scan Y/N
5/56
Move on

Day 6: Reflect & Recharge

This week we focused on waking up, experiencing the here and now, and becoming more aware of our experiences as they unfold. We practised noticing one small thing and using the body scan as a means of developing the mind-body connection.

Please now complete the following:

Week 1 Reflections

What did you take away from this week's activities?

_____

_____

_____

_____

_____
_____
_____
_____

What are you grateful for?

_____
_____
_____
_____

What were the 3 highlights of the week and which made you happy?

1._____

_____

2._____

_____

3._____

_____

Complete Y
+Body scan Y/N
6/56
Move on to Day 7

Day 7 Rest & Reward

Congratulations on making it to the end of the first week on the road to optimal well-being. Stay with me it does take a little time to reap the benefits. Take time out today to rest. Remember: we all need to slow down in order to speed up.

Before you move on to Week 2, please take the time to reward yourself with a treat. For example, a meal with friends, a small purchase, or simply by reminding yourself of the progress you have made.

Week 1 Reward: And Breathe....

My reward to myself for putting my well-being at the heart of what I do will be:

_____

_____

_____

_____

Complete Y

7/56

Move on to Week 2

WEEK 2 THEME – COMING TO OUR SENSES

Day 1 Insight

Day 2 Mind-body connector (7/11 breathing)

Day 3 Fitness habit-breaker (take a breath)

Day 4 Nutrition habit-breaker (take a breath)

Day 5 Health habit-breaker (take a breath)

Day 6 Reflect & Recharge

Day 7 Rest & reward

###

Day 1 Insight:

"The ultimate expression of humility comes when we control our senses."

—Radhanath Swami

Well done on getting to Week 2. This really is an achievement, as it's very easy with mindfulness to say it's not for me as it's so alien to what you are used to. Many people find the first week the hardest. I do hope you found last week's mindfulness activities useful (and perhaps are trying to add practice to your daily routine or simply notice that you're not practising!).

You may have encountered that things get in the way with your practice. Many people find it hard to initiate a daily mindfulness practice and often find it difficult to be mindful in the way they go about their day. Please don't worry: this is perfectly normal. The Buddhist monks have practiced for thousands of years and they still say they have more to learn.

You may also find it awkward; you may feel bored or anxious at first; you may even feel disappointed that the benefits of mindfulness aren't instant. For many people, mind wandering during activities or overthinking during the activities are also common difficulties.

Please trust me and stay with it. Mindfulness teaches us that the best things in life are worth waiting for! The key objective is just to practice, notice your thoughts, feelings, and observations about the practice, but avoid being too critical. Remind yourself that you bought this book because you thought it might help you improve your well-being. It's like any new habit that is difficult to master: you don't have to like it; you just have to do it, it comes with practice! The most important thing is to keep going, persevere, and stay hopeful.

If you find that you're not doing the practices or it's sporadic, try not to be too judgemental (Remember that an important aspect of mindfulness is to begin to challenge that inner critic of yours). Use any opportunity to notice your grenades (overthinking) and return to your sensations.

This week is about expanding our waking up and coming to our senses with more purpose and understanding. There are two main ways in which our minds tend to operate: we either *experience the world* or *conceptualise the world*.

Our direct experience of the world relates to what we see, hear, touch, etc. (primary experience). Our conceptualization of the world is related to the way we label every experience and then think about, analyse, compare, judge it, etc. (secondary experience).

On the surface, there is nothing wrong with our minds operating both experientially and conceptually, until we end up overusing one at the expense of the other. When you're stressed, the mind tends to over-conceptualise, which amounts to excessive worrying, analysing, problem-solving, etc. The ability to think, analyse, and reflect is a wonderful thing, but when we're stressed, we tend to overdo it like an iPod on repeat, and this mental activity tends to keep us trapped in ever growing feelings of stress. The more stressed we become, the more we tend to engage in past and future thinking.

The problem with this is that our memories give us very unreliable information on what really happened—remember, these memories are only your perception of what happened and not necessarily the true narrative. The greater challenge here is the more we try to remember, the less accurate it gets. This means that rumination of past and future thinking are taking up our valuable energy and to little benefit.

We may also notice with time that thinking often takes us away from fully attending to and taking in what is in front of us, therefore creating absence and disconnection. The only real thing that matters is the here and now! Mindfulness practice helps us to move towards lowering our conceptualising and to become immersed with a more direct experience of the world, less doing and more being. This involves less thinking or ruminating on past and future experiences. The great thing about mindfulness is we don't have to make an effort to think less: our attention is so taken up with direct sensory experience that there's simply no room left in our mind for thinking about much else.

The Paradox of Mindfulness

At the heart of mindfulness practice lies a paradox: if you want to move from conceptual thought to experience the present, you have to really be in the here and now!

Let's say you want to get from a state of tension to calm, for instance. What we really need to do is simply feel the tension rather than making efforts to stop feeling tense and start feeling calm (which tends to make us feel more tense!), The more we explore and stay curious about our feelings by encouraging a state of being rather than doing the more experiential it becomes.

Habit-breaker Exercise

This week's habit-breaker is to do something really simple: focus on one of the most powerful things we possess, our *breathing!* The aim is to do something in a more deliberate fashion, more slowly, and with more sensory attention (sound, movement, body sensations, e.g., your chest rising, how it feels to be immersed in the here and now) than usual. Take one simple, **fully connected breath**, on purpose.

Focus on connecting to its sensation (primary/sensory experience) as fully as you can, noticing its flow, depth, sound and flavour. Feed your brain with a simple moment of a full, undivided refreshment on sensory attention. Then repeat this a few times, at will, on purpose, without attaching judgement to it.

Look out for the sensations in the moment. This is a good way to inhibit the tendency we have to suddenly career off and mind-wander into the past and future. If you are aware of thoughts distracting your sensory experience, then go back to the breath!

Day 1 Activity: Take a Breath

Today's observations:

_____

_____

_____

_____

_____

_____

_____

_____

_____

Complete Y
8/56
Move on

Day 2 Mind-body Connector

This week we will ask you to practice a new mind-body connector (a mindfulness technique designed to develop the mind-body connection). This week is the **7/11 breathing** technique and is usually done lying down, although you can also do it sitting up. This simple breathing exercise is a fantastic technique to use if you start to feel stressed during the day. Instead of continuing to feel overwhelmed, breathing will help you to feel better prepared to deal with the stressors as they arise. If possible, aim to practice this breathing technique outside surrounded by nature.

The *7/11 technique* is a breathing exercise where you breathe in for a count of 7 and out for a count 11. It is used to help you relax and gain/regain composure in a variety of situations.

1. Find somewhere comfortable to sit and relax.

2. Sit in a chair with your shoulders relaxed and your hands folded gently over your tummy.

3. If possible, breathe in and out through your nose. In for a count of 7 and out for a count of 11. (If you find it too hard to breathe out 11, start off with 3/6 and work up to 7/11. The important thing here is to breathe out longer than you breathe in.)

4. If you are doing it correctly, your shoulders will remain still and your tummy will get bigger and smaller as you breathe (called belly or diaphragmatic breathing).

5. Once you can keep your shoulders still and relaxed without effort, it is a good idea to close your eyes and try to picture the numbers in your mind's eye, to help you concentrate completely on your breathing.

###

Day 2 Activity: 7/11 Breathing

Today's observations:

_____

_____

_____

_____

_____

_____

_____

_____

_____

Complete Y
9/56
Move on

NOW AIM TO PRACTICE THE MIND-BODY CONNECTOR 7/11 BREATHING TECHNIQUE EVERY DAY FOR THE REST OF THE WEEK ALONGSIDE YOUR DAILY ACTIVITY.

Day 3 Fitness Habit-breaker

Today we are going to practice what you learned at the start of the week, by using **one fully connected breath** with a *focus on fitness*. The key objective in this exercise is to ensure that whatever fitness exercise you chose, e.g., a stretch, jogging, squats, you try to do it using the power of a single breath outlined in Day 1.

Pay attention to how the exercise feels, including any changes in your breathing, what muscle groups you sense, etc. Use the breath as the anchor to your senses, encouraging you to fill the lungs with air during the exercise. If you find your mind wanders, gently acknowledge this and go back to the breath! Select an exercise and record it below.

Day 3 Activity: Fitness – Take a breath

Exercise:

_____

_____

Today's observations:

_____

_____

_____

_____

_____

_____

_____

Complete Y
7/11 breathing Y/N
10/56
Move on

Day 4 Nutrition Habit-breaker

Today we are going to practice what you learned at the start of the week by using **one fully connected breath** with a *focus on nutrition.* The key objective in this exercise is to ensure that whatever piece of food you choose, e.g., one piece of chocolate, one strawberry, one grape, that you eat it mindfully, using the same technique outlined in Day 1.

Pay attention to the breath as you eat. Use the breath as an anchor to the senses, encouraging you to not rush your food and to enjoy the experience.

If you find your mind wanders, gently acknowledge this and go back to the breath! Select a food choice and record it below.

Day 4 Activity: Nutrition – Take a breath

Food choice:

_____

_____

Today's observations:

_____

_____

_____

_____

_____

_____

_____

Complete Y
7/11 breathing Y/N
11/56
Move on

Day 5 Health Habit-breaker

Science persuades us of the power of nature. It is something we intuitively understand but may not utilise enough. Research shows that spending time in natural spaces has considerable benefits for mental and physical health.

Today we are going to practice what you learned at the start of the week by using **one fully connected breath** whilst being connected with nature. Whether you chose to sit somewhere comfortable outside, go for a walk on your break, or join a friend for a dog walk, pay attention to the breath as you take in the experience.

Use the breath as an anchor to the senses, e.g., sounds, smells, and touch, encouraging you to not rush your breath and enjoy the experience. If you find your mind wanders, gently acknowledge this and go back to the breath. Select an outside location to practice this and record it below.

Day 5 Activity: Health – Take a breath

Source of nature:

_____

_____

Today's observations:

_____

_____

_____

_____

_____

_____

Complete Y
7/11 breathing Y/N
12/56
Move on

Day 6 Reflect & Recharge

This week, we focused on coming to our senses by using the breath as our anchor to experience the here and now and to become more aware of our experiences as they unfold. We practised using the breath to come back to the senses when the mind wanders, and using the breath as a means of developing the mind-body connection.

Please now complete the following:

Week 2 Reflections

What did you take away from this week's activities?

_____

_____

_____

_____

_____

_____

_____

_____

What are you grateful for?

_____

_____

_____

_____

_____

What were the 3 highlights of the week and which made you happy?

1._____

_____

_____

2._____

_____

_____

3._____

_____

_____

Complete Y
7/11 breathing Y/N
13/56
Move on to Day 7

Day 7 Rest & Reward

Congratulations on making it to the end of the second week on the road to optimal well-being. Don't forget to take time out today to rest, see friends and generally enjoy downtime.

Before you move on to Week 3, please take the time to reward yourself with a treat. For example, a meal with friends, a small purchase, or simply by reminding yourself of the progress you have made.

Week 2 Reward: And Breathe....

My reward to myself for putting my well-being at the heart of what I do will be:

_____

_____

_____

_____

_____

Complete Y
14/56
Move on to Week 3

WEEK 3: THEME – MINDFULNESS OF THOUGHT

Day 1 Insight

Day 2 Mind-body connector (the 3-minute break)

Day 3 Fitness habit-breaker (the bus stop)

Day 4 Nutrition (habit-breaker (the bus stop)

Day 5 Health (habit-breaker (the bus stop)

Day 6 Reflect & Recharge

Day 7 Rest & reward

Day 1 Insight

"All that we are is the result of what we have thought."

—Buddha

One of the most powerful observations people often notice when they first start to practice mindfulness is just how many thoughts coincide with everything they do. You may have become more aware that the mind appears to never switch off from thought. Some people even conclude that the practice of mindfulness is making them think more than they ever were before they started practicing. This is in fact not true! It is just that by awakening and coming to your senses, you are beginning to notice just how busy the mind is and, therefore, have a better opportunity to respond in a novel way to the internal "grenades" going off in your head.

A common myth about mindfulness is that the end goal is to "make the mind vacant" or to "empty the mind" or "to feel nothingness" and anything short of this isn't mindfulness. That is as true as thinking that as long as you eat a takeaway every day before 6 p.m., you will avoid piling on weight!

Rather, in mindfulness practice, we attempt to look and analyse our thoughts rather than run away from them. Usually, when we have a thought, we don't tend to question it, we tend to believe what it on face value, and we then look at the world from the point of view of that thought and perspective!

Of course, it's not that *everything* we think is untrue. It's just that not everything we think *is* true, just because you have accepted it as so. Likewise, not everything we think is helpful to us. Remember back to our inner critic, as being our own worst enemy. Mindfulness helps us to notice our thoughts without necessarily taking them as an absolute truth, without "buying into them" or accepting to go along with a thought.

This is often harder than it first seems and made more or less challenging by the nature of the thought you are having. Some thoughts are fairly trivial, so they don't have a strong emotional "pull"—such as "What shall I have for dinner today?" It's quite easy to notice such a thought and then let it go. Other thoughts, in contrast, are much more serious in nature, emotionally loaded, and have a sense of importance about them—such as "I shouldn't stay in this relationship."

The Value of Objective Thinking

I am not saying that thinking is to be avoided and a bad thing, or that it doesn't have much value and so you should just ignore all thoughts and let them go. Far from it! Thinking is necessary to help us to have a productive and fulfilled life and it can be immensely valuable if it is fully mindful, managed, positive, even perhaps creative, and most of all objective.

To think something through objectively, to question its truth, to come to a conclusion, if possible, or at least muddle it over is an important life skill to master. For instance, we may have a decision to make that requires us to think about the possible consequences in following through a certain course of action, such as, "Shall I change health club?"

In trying to think this through, we will probably become aware of trains of thought that distract us from our task. In that case, our object of focus would be the thoughts connected with the possibility of moving clubs. The other thoughts that "intrude" upon this topic we can deal with in the way we have recommended above: simply notice them and let them go.

Engaging in too many thoughts can result in paralysis by analysis and will get us stuck trying to "solve" too much. This effectively may result in us doing nothing, and tunnel vision may ensue as a result of feeling overwhelmed. This doesn't help our decision making, when you need to be aware not only of your thinking but of all options open to you.

Habit-breaker Exercise

So, what's your choice? Will you carry on going on every possible journey and potentially get stuck? Or will you be aware of multiple lines of thoughts (potential "land mines") and choose which "journeys" to take and which to let go of?

Imagine you are at a bus stop, sitting on a seat, and buses are coming past. Which bus will you get on and which one will you let pass you? This week's habit-breaker is to learn to appreciate the value of objective thinking using the bus stop and the following 8-part process:

* Bring yourself into the present moment.
* Acknowledge and register your experience, even if it is unwanted or unpleasant.
* Gently bring your full attention to breathing, to breathing in and breathing out as they follow.
* Grow the field of awareness around your breathing, to come to your senses and use the body as a whole as your sensory awareness seat (the buss stop).
* Notice thoughts coming and going like buses pulling up at a bus stop. Notice the "appealing" thoughts/images and ones not so.
* Now choose: Will you travel on it? Will you fight it? Or will you acknowledge it—pleasant or unpleasant—and let it go?
* Just like being at a bus stop, some journeys are unwanted or not worth going on. Stay with a

detached awareness as you pick and choose your thoughts.

✳ Remember to return to the bus stop—your sensory awareness seat—each time you become distracted.

Day 1 Activity: The Bus Stop

Today's observations:

_____

_____

_____

_____

_____

_____

_____

Complete Y
15/56
Move on

Day 2 Mind-Body Connector

Ask yourself: Do you ever stop for a moment with whatever you are doing and take a break? An authentic break, as in do nothing, absolutely nothing?

So many people go mindlessly from one activity to another throughout the day, not even taking a break for lunch or they eat their lunch whilst they work—so effective! Does this sound like you?

It's great to have a productive day, but going about our day void of any breaks isn't healthy. It keeps us suspended in *doing* mode and is a major source of stress. Living in a world where we are constantly connected has made this problem even worse. The worrying thing is constant connection is a habit that makes it increasingly harder to switch off and do nothing. We feel obliged to do rather than be.

This week, I invite you to take a **3-minute break** each day. A *few* 3-minute breaks throughout your day would be even better if you can spare that much time in your busy diary? I would argue, as a means of avoiding the impact of stress, you can't afford *not* to!

Research tells us overwhelmingly that we are more productive when we take frequent short breaks. When we are constantly on the go, things become more chaotic and we become drained, our minds get tired, and we end up paying less attention to the task in hand. Consequently, we don't do as good a job as we're capable of. A paradox being that taking regular breaks, in the end, makes us more efficient!

Day 2 Activity: Take a break

Number of breaks: _____

Length of breaks: _____

Today's observations:

_____

_____

_____

_____

_____

_____

_____

_____

Complete Y
16/56
Move on

NOW AIM TO PRACTICE TAKING A BREAK EVERY DAY ALONGSIDE YOUR DAILY ACTIVITY.

Day 3 Fitness Habit-breaker

Today we are going to practice what you learned at the start of the week by using the **bus stop** with a *focus on fitness*. The key objective in this exercise is to ensure that whatever fitness exercise you chose, e.g., walking, running, an exercise class, that you try something challenging using the power of the bus stop technique outlined in Day 1.

Use the bus stop as the anchor to your senses, encouraging you to redirect focus back to the exercise when your brain wanders. If you find your mind wanders, gently acknowledge this and get back to the bus stop!

When you experience negative and positive thoughts about the exercise, choose which you will hold on to and which you won't. Aim to hold on to positive thoughts, like, "I am enjoying this," "this feels good," and let go of thoughts like, "This is too hard, this isn't fun." Select an exercise and record it below.

Day 3 Activity: Fitness – The bus stop

Exercise:

_____

_____

_____

Today's observations:

_____

_____

_____

_____

_____

_____

_____

_____

_____

Complete Y
The 3-minute break Y/N
17/56
Move on

Day 4 Nutrition Habit-breaker

Today we are going to practice what you learned at the start of the week by using the **bus stop** with a *focus on nutrition.* The key objective in this exercise is to consider your relationship with food using the same technique outlined in Day 1.

Use the bus stop as the anchor to your senses, encouraging you to redirect focus back to the senses when your brain wanders. If you find your mind wanders, gently acknowledge this and get back to the bus stop!

When you experience negative and positive thoughts about your nutrition, choose which you will hold on to and which you won't. Aim to hold on to positive thought like, "I am making progress with my nutrition," "I can begin to be at peace with food," and let go of thoughts like, "This is too hard, I will never lose weight."

Day 4 Activity: Nutrition – The bus stop

Relationship with food?

_____

_____

_____

_____

_____

_____

_____

Today's observations:

_____

_____

_____

_____

_____

_____

_____

Complete Y
The 3-minute break Y/N
18/56
Move on

Day 5 Health Habit-breaker

Research shows us that a good sleep routine helps us to feel calmer and more energised. It also helps to combat depression, shrink your waistline, improve your focus and productivity at work, regulate your hormones, boost your immunity, and so much more. But the power of sleep in enabling the body to heal itself is often wasted by negative thoughts running through the mind.

The key objective in this exercise is to use the breath to ease yourself into a relaxed state for sleep and to use the **bus stop** as the anchor to your senses. Encourage yourself to redirect focus back to senses when your brain wanders. If you find your mind wanders, gently acknowledge this and get back to the bus stop! If you find your mind continues to wander, gently acknowledge this and, rather than lying awake worried you will forget, write it down and allow the thought to pass!

Day 5 Activity: Health – The bus stop

Today's observations:

_____

_____

_____

_____

_____

_____

_____

Complete Y
The 3-minute break Y/N
19/56
Move on

Day 6 Reflect & Recharge

This week we focused on the value of objective thinking by using the bus stop as our anchor to experiencing the here and now, becoming more aware of our experiences as they unfold, and deciding which thoughts to hold on to and accept and which thoughts to let go of. We practised using a break to come back to the senses as a means of developing the mind-body connection.

Please now complete the following:

Week 3 Reflections

What did you take away from this week's activities?

_____

_____

_____

_____

_____

_____

_____

_____

What are you grateful for?

_____

_____

_____

_____

_____

_____

What were the 3 highlights of the week and which made you happy?

1._____

_____

_____

_____

2._____

_____

_____

3._____

_____

_____

Complete Y
The 3-minute break Y/N
20/56
Move on to Day 7

Day 7 Rest & Reward

Congratulations on making it to the end of the third week on the road to optimal well-being. Take time out today to rest—you are more than a third of the way there already.

Before you move on to Week 4, please take the time to reward yourself with a treat, e.g., a meal with friends, a small purchase or simply by reminding yourself of the progress you have made.

Week 3 Reward: And Breathe....

My reward to myself for putting my well-being at the heart of what I do will be:

_____

_____

_____

Complete Y
21/56
Move on to Week 4

WEEK 4: THEME – EMBRACING DIFFICULTY

Day 1 Insight

Day 2 Mind-body connector (mindful movement)

Day 3 Fitness habit-breaker (a learned acceptance)

Day 4 Nutrition habit-breaker (a learned acceptance)

Day 5 Health habit-breaker (a learned acceptance)

Day 6 Reflect & Recharge

Day 7 Rest & Reward

###

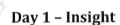 **Day 1 – Insight**

"Never give up, for that is just the place and time that the tide will turn."

—Harriet Beecher Stowe

It is human nature to seek pleasure and avoid pain. However, we can't possibly live our lives without going through difficult experiences, it's impossible to avoid them. Everyone's life has experiences that are difficult, unbearable, troubled, or even painful, as well as easy, satisfying, delightful and enjoyable ones. The art of optimal living doesn't consist of trying to avoid all the difficult experiences and accept only the easy ones, but instead learning how to respond rather than react to the inevitable ups and downs that life puts in our path.

Acceptance doesn't mean merely handling or living with difficulty with unflappable resilience. It's much more active than this. When you find out what it *feels* like, this gets somewhat close to what we mean by acceptance—willingness to have the experience, to feel it with all our senses.

It's natural to shy away from suffering, to harden ourselves against it, to protect ourselves from it. While this can be a good strategy for some things, if this is always our habitual default position, we will tend to become cold-hearted towards life— unfortunately, the good as well as the bad. Accepting a stressful experience means to touch it, feel its makeup, its brokenness, its discomfort. If you can learn to do this, you'll probably notice you're experiencing the good things in life more fully, in technicolour rather than black and white.

Learning how to accept difficult experiences strengthens our tolerance in dealing with stress and our resolve. That is, we learn how to experience them without them rubbing us up the wrong way. Rather, we have the means to be with difficult situations and emotions in a calm, responsible, proactive way, instead of reacting to them. It doesn't consist of hardening yourself to these experiences; it's more about limiting your reaction to them. People with a high degree of stress tolerance feel the discomfort, but acknowledge it for what it is.

The next time you find yourself stressed, first of all simply notice that it's happening and that it's unpleasant. See if you can *be* with the unpleasant experience with openness and acceptance, without reacting to it.

Acknowledge that it's tough, that it's an experience that hurts. This is an important lesson to learn. You might even say to yourself, "This is a moment of distress." Try not to beat yourself up about it. Have self-compassion and empathy for what you are going through, just like you would for a friend or loved one who is having a tough time. Kindly, considerately, gently, and with love. After all, you're doing something burdensome.

Habit-breaker Exercise

This week's habit-breaker is to see if you can be with a difficult situation and accept it, rather than fight against it. It's probably best to start practising with something relatively mild, like being caught in heavy traffic or stuck late at a meeting; having to do something you'd rather not be doing; or being upset with someone's conduct. Once you've had some practice in being with relatively mild experiences, you can move onto more difficult ones.

Using the breath can help. Take your attention to it, especially as you feel it lower down in your body. Feel your abdomen swelling and subsiding.

You can imagine breathing into the unpleasant experience, and, on the out-breath, see if you can let go of your resistance to what's happening.

Try to allow the difficult situation to simply be there, just as it is, without your needing to do anything about it. See if you can hold it in your attention in a soft, gentle, calm way.

Breathing in the experience, breathing out the resistance. Breathing in the discomfort, breathing out kindness to yourself.

###

Day 1 Activity: A Learned Acceptance

Difficult Experience:

_____

_____

_____

_____

_____

_____

Today's observations:

_____

_____

_____

_____

_____

_____

_____

_____

_____

_____

Complete Y
22/56
Move on

Day 2 Mind-Body Connector

This week, we will ask you to practice a new mind-body connector: **mindful movement**.

Mindful movement is about becoming aware of your senses insofar as they are a reflection of your thoughts. You did do mindful movement in week 1, when you did one small thing for exercise. If your body is tight and rigid your thoughts probably are, too. Likewise, if your body is relaxed and calm, so may your thoughts be.

Very few of us listen to what our body is telling us when in actual fact it is a great barometer to show us how we are, as opposed to how we think we are. By using mindful movement, you can train yourself how to use the body as an anchor, something to come back to you when your mind starts to work overtime.

Regardless of the exercise you choose, try to stay with the sensation of the movement. Notice when you're making too much effort or if you're tensing any other part of the body. Use your breath to help you focus on the movement. Come back to neutral and become conscious of the effects the exercise has had. Let the focus go…

Day 2 Activity: Mindful Movement

Exercise choice:

_____

_____

_____

Today's observations:

_____

_____

_____

_____

_____

_____

_____

_____

Complete Y
23/56
Move on

NOW AIM TO PRACTICE THE MINDFUL MOVEMENT TECHNIQUE EVERY DAY FOR THE REST OF THE WEEK ALONGSIDE YOUR DAILY ACTIVITY.

Day 3 Fitness Habit-breaker

Today we are going to practice what you learned at the start of the week by **learning to accept** something difficult with a *focus on fitness*. The key objective in this exercise is to ensure that whatever fitness exercise you chose, e.g., strength work, cardio workout, stretching, that you select something you have always found difficult and try to do it using the learned acceptance method outlined in Day 1.

Pay attention to how the exercise feels, as you accept that it is difficult. Use the breath as the anchor to your senses, encouraging you to fill the lungs with air during the exercise. If you find your mind telling you how difficult it is, gently acknowledge this and go back to the breath!

Select an exercise and record it below.

Day 3 Activity: Fitness – A Learned Acceptance

Exercise:

_____

_____

_____

Today's observations:

_____

_____

_____

_____

_____

_____

_____

_____

Complete Y
Mindful movement Y/N
24/56
Move on

Day 4 Nutrition Habit-breaker

Today we are going to practice what you learned at the start of the week by **learning to accept** something difficult with a *focus on nutrition.* The key objective in this exercise is to ensure that whatever nutrition habit you choose, e.g. pre-preparing your food, not eating after 6 p.m., not overeating, that you select something you have always found difficult and try to do it using the learned acceptance method outlined in Day 1.

Pay attention to how it feels, as you accept that it is difficult. Use the breath as the anchor to your senses, encouraging you to fill the lungs with air during the exercise. If you find your mind is telling you how difficult it is, gently acknowledge this and go back to the breath!

Select a habit and record it below.

Day 4 Activity: Nutrition – A Learned Acceptance

Nutrition habit:

_____

_____

_____

Today's observations:

_____

_____

_____

_____

_____

_____

_____

Complete Y
Mindful movement Y/N
25/56
Move on

Day 5 Health Habit-breaker

Today we are going to practice what you learned at the start of the week by **learning to accept** something difficult with a *focus on health*. The key objective in this exercise is to ensure that whatever health habit you chose, e.g., sleep, not having a drink or smoke, select something you have always found difficult and try to do it using the learned acceptance method outlined in Day 1.

Pay attention to how it feels, as you accept that it is difficult. Use the breath as the anchor to your senses, encouraging you to fill the lungs with air during the exercise. If you find your mind telling you how difficult it is, gently acknowledge this and go back to the breath!

Select a habit and record it below.

Day 5 Activity: Health – A Learned Acceptance

Health habit:

_____

_____

_____

_____

Today's observations:

_____

_____

_____

_____

_____

_____

_____

_____

_____

Complete Y
Mindful movement Y/N
26/56
Move on

Day 6 Reflect & Recharge

This week we focused on coming to our senses by embracing difficulty and using our learned acceptance technique to get comfortable with good and bad experiences. We also used mindful movement as a means of coming back to the senses and understanding how our thoughts affect our body as a means of developing the mind-body connection.

Please now complete the following:

Week 4 Reflections

What did you take away from this week's activities?

_____

_____

_____

_____

_____

_____

_____

_____

_____

What are you grateful for?

_____

_____

_____

_____

_____

_____

What were the 3 highlights of the week and which made you happy?

1._____

_____

_____

2._____

_____

_____

3._____

_____

_____

Complete Y
Mindful movement Y/N
27/56
Move on to Day 7

Day 7 Rest & Reward

Congratulations on making it to the end of the fourth week on the road to optimal well-being. You are halfway there. Take time out today to rest. Remember the power of slowing down in order to speed up.

Before you move on to Week 5, please take the time to reward yourself with a treat, e.g., a meal with friends, a small purchase, or simply by reminding yourself of the progress you have made.

Week 4 Reward: And Breathe....

My reward to myself for putting my well-being at the heart of what I do will be:

_____

_____

_____

_____

_____

_____

Complete Y
28/56
Move on to Week 5

WEEK 5: THEME – THE JOY OF THE GREEN CICRLE

Day 1 Insight

Day 2 Mind-body connector (loving kindness meditation)

Day 3 Fitness habit-breaker (self-kindness)

Day 4 Nutrition habit-breaker (self-kindness)

Day 5 Health habit-breaker (self-kindness)

Day 6 Reflect & Recharge

Day 7 Rest & Reward

###

 Day 1 Insight

"Perhaps we should love ourselves so fiercely that when others see us they know exactly how it should be done."

—Rudy Francisco

Managing your emotions is one of the most challenging behaviours we face as humans and one of the best ways to avoid stress and build resilience in ourselves. Daniel Goleman refers to one's ability to regulate their thoughts, feelings, and emotions as *emotional intelligence*, and it is a vital regulatory capacity that we must master, if we are to have fulfilling relationships with ourselves and others.

We have three main in-built systems that help us to do this:

> The *threat* system (red circle), which is designed to help us recognise and avoid danger
> The *achieving* system (blue circle), which drives us to get the good things in life and rewards us when we succeed, and
> The *soothing* system (green circle), which plays an important role when we're not in danger and when we've got everything we need right now to survive.

For most people, stress is the result of spending too much time in the red and/or blue circles. This week is designed to address this and recalibrate helping you find joy by spending more time in the green circle.

The emotions in this system include appreciation, relaxation, contentment, satisfaction, fun, playfulness, affection, empathy, kindness, love, compassion, and happiness. The green circle is essentially in the *being* mode of mind, whereas the red and blue circles are associated as the *doing* mode of mind. It is fair to deduce that we spend too much time doing and not enough time being, but at what cost?

There is good scientific reason to spend more time in the green circle. This relates to chemicals the brain releases depending on the type of experiences you have. When we live in constant flight or fight (the red circle) and feel threatened, our brain releases the stress hormone cortisol, which is useful for short-term defensive behaviour because it mobilises fats, energises the body, and focuses attention. However, when cortisol levels remain elevated for too long, it can damage the immune system and the brain.

Likewise, if we spend too long in the blue circle chasing achievement, the pleasant feelings it elicits and resulting boost of dopamine can ultimately become quite addictive. Over the long term, this can lead to overworking and, ultimately, burnout.

It's amazing how we often don't see the danger in living like this—it's not healthy for a body to have drugs such as cocaine and heroin, we get this message! So why don't we see the danger in the body being constantly overdosed with chemicals associated with high levels of stress? The long and short of it is stress isn't a silent killer like people say. The answer lies in cortisol and that is very visible to a GP!

Spending more time in the soothing system (green circle) results in our feeling safe, content, and peaceful as endorphins are released into our body. Contentment and its absence of striving or wanting; results in an inner peacefulness that is quite different from the hyped-up excitement of the "striving and succeeding" feeling of the achieving system. It is a form of being happy with the way things are.

The key takeaway here is that stress builds at an alarming rate when these three systems are out of balance, and especially when the threat and/or the achieving systems continue to be aroused and don't switch off even when not required. This makes us habitually feel worried, frazzled, hassled, and rushed, resulting in our brains being in the same state of arousal as a man running away from the snake in the grass! When we're not stressed out trying to keep up with the demands of our life we're trying to get some new thing that we hope will make us feel good.

It's not that these emotions are altogether bad: after all we need them to protect us from danger and to motivate us to seek the good things in life. It's just, when they get out of hand, they can make us very unhappy.

Our frantic paced lives tend to encourage us to live too much of our lives in the first two systems and largely neglect the third. The practice of mindfulness helps us to find some balance between these systems, specifically by developing and nurturing the soothing and contentment system. The hormone oxytocin is connected with our feelings of connectedness and, with the endorphins, gives us the feelings of well-being that flow from feeling loved, wanted, and safe with others.

Engaging in kindness mediation, which uses this system, is really important in helping us feeling connected to ourselves and others.

Spending time in the green circle is a great way to maintain awareness, connect with the situation, and have the flexibility to use drive or threat when they work, but also to step back when they do not. There is real joy to be had from spending time in the green circle!

Research on kindness, which is "an attitude of care and concern for the well-being of others and of ourselves," is proving to be a very important aspect in developing the soothing system. Cultivating kindness in the holistic sense includes sympathy or concern for our own and others' well-being plus a willingness to act on that concern. This is central to the meaning behind this book. If you are kind to yourself in terms of your well-being and you are willing to act, then you are halfway there.

In its purest form, kindness to oneself may be as simple as indulging oneself to be fully connected to the present, granting oneself a regular break, allowing oneself a gesture of self-compassion through directed loving kindness.

When someone isn't kind to you and is overly critical of you (like what happened to me in my toxic relationship), your stress hormone—cortisol—will increase. That person's unpleasantness towards you may make you feel anxious, upset, or unhappy because the threat system in your brain has been triggered. If their criticism is harsh and constant over a long period of time, it becomes very difficult to switch the threat response off. Even when the person isn't being particularly unkind to you, you will remain on red alert. You may well become distressed, unhappy, or depressed, which is what happened in my case.

The interesting thing here is that our own "inner critic" works in much the same way and can have the same toxic effect. If you are constantly unkind to yourself and put yourself down, this also activates the *threat system* in your brain, making you feel anxious, angry, and stressed. Our own thoughts can affect the parts of our brain that give rise to stressful and unpleasant feelings. They can certainly tone down positive feelings. We don't feel joy, happiness, well-being, or contentment when being criticised. If we allow our inner-critic to dominate our mind then we are constantly on a danger setting and this will understandably not feel too nice.

Alternatively, suppose that there is someone who cares about you, when things are difficult, they understand how tough it is, and encourage you with genuine love and concern. It indeed feels great! When someone is kind and supportive, and encouraging towards us, the hormone oxytocin is stimulated, and we feel soothed and calmed.

If we deliberately learn to be kind and supportive to ourselves and others by giving helpful mind messages when things are hard, we are more likely to stimulate those parts of the brain that respond to kindness. This will help us cope with stress and set-backs because we are recalibrating the emotional systems in our brain. There is now a lot of evidence that self-kindness and self-compassion (kindness to ourselves when we are suffering) are associated with well-being and the ability to cope with life's stresses. The same goes for others: if we are kind to others, they respond in a positive way.

Our brains by natures design need and respond positively to kindness, granted it needs more reinforcement to sink in. It's not any different than training your body to be fit and healthy: we need to train our mind to be fit and healthy, too. It's simply developing the habit of treating our brain kindly and feeding it with positivity, i.e., *good brain nutrition.* This is no different to understanding that our body needs certain macros and micros in a balanced diet. We just need to understand how our mind works and then practice how to fuel it with things to make it work optimally.

Habit-breaker exercise

So, this week you're invited to spend some time in the green circle every day. There are so many ways of doing this. Here are just a few examples:

* Have fun each and every day. Be playful. Don't be so serious with yourself.
* Take time to enjoy all the facilities at the gym, e.g., shower, sauna and café, rather than rushing through.
* Be fully present when you're talking to someone—a friend, colleague, or family member, even a stranger—try to connect with them by giving them your whole attention. Listen to them in all that they're saying and doing.
* Do something you really enjoy and that requires your full attention. Something that makes you concentrate on a task to the exclusion of all other distractions. This may be your hobby, something you do for its own sake.
* Make someone's day by engaging in random acts of kindness!
* Tell someone what you like and admire about them.

There are so many other ways of entering the green circle, so don't confine yourself to the above examples. Be creative! Enjoy yourself.

Day 1 Activity: Loving Kindness

Today's observations:

_____

_____

_____

_____

_____

_____

_____

_____

Complete Y
29/56
Move on

Day 2 Mind-body connector

Today we are going to do a new mind-body connector with a focus on a **loving kindness meditation**. Actually developing self-compassion is so important that bringing loving kindness into your daily life is a focus on both the connectors and the habit-breakers for the entire week.

Begin by sitting comfortably in a quiet place fully prepared and ready to start a meditation on fostering loving kindness. In order to open yourself to healthy relationships, kindness, and connection to others, it first begins with showing kindness to yourself—otherwise known as *self-compassion.*

Think of a quality or attribute you appreciate about yourself, that you are proud of, in order to feel positive about yourself. Take it in and contemplate this for a while.

Now identify some positive intentions for yourself. For example, I will be healthy, I will have positive mental health, I will be happy.

Repeat whatever phrases come from your heart and flow into your mind that feel powerful to you—that have deep meaning for you.

Once you feel the positivity that flows from adopting a kind approach to yourself, you can pay this good feeling forward to others. Bring up a visual image of someone you love or care about and pass on these positive wishes you afforded on yourself to them, too.

Record below any feelings of kindness, compassion, and connection that arise from your starting point of self-love and self-compassion.

Day 2 Activity: Loving Kindness Meditation

Duration of meditation: _____

Today's observations:

_____

_____

_____

_____

_____

_____

_____

_____

_____

_____

_____

Complete Y
30/56
Move on

NOW AIM TO PRACTICE THE LOVING KINDNESS MEDITATION TECHNIQUE EVERY DAY FOR THE REST OF THE WEEK ALONGSIDE YOUR DAILY ACTIVITY.

Day 3 Fitness habit-breaker

Today we are going to practice what you learned at the start of the week by using **loving kindness** with a *focus on fitness*. The key objective in this exercise is to ensure that whatever fitness exercise you chose, e.g., go for a walk, a run, take an exercise class, doing squats, it should be something you absolutely love. Use loving kindness by showing yourself self-compassion.

Think of a quality or attribute you bring to your fitness sessions and something you are proud of that you are achieving with your fitness. Contemplate it for a while. Now identify some positive intentions before the session begins—may this session be great!

Repeat the phrase a few times and visualise a great session before you start.

Select an exercise and record it below.

Day 3 Activity: Fitness – Loving Kindness

Exercise:

_____

_____

_____

Today's observations:

_____

_____

_____

_____

_____

_____

_____

_____

_____

Complete Y
Meditation Y/N
31/56
Move on

Day 4 Nutrition habit-breaker

Today we are going to practice what you learned at the start of the week by using **loving kindness** with a *focus on nutrition*. The key objective in this exercise is to ensure that whatever nutrition habit you chose—e.g., preparing a meal, selecting a healthy choice, or avoiding overeating—you do it with self-love. Use loving kindness by showing yourself self-compassion.

Think of a quality or attribute you bring to your nutrition and something you are proud of that you are achieving with your nutrition. Contemplate it for a while. Now identify some positive intentions before you begin—may this experience be great! Repeat the phrase a few times and visualise a great experience before you start. Select a nutrition habit and record it below.

Day 4 Activity: Nutrition – Loving Kindness

Nutrition habit:

_____

_____

Today's observations:

_____

_____

_____

_____

_____

_____

_____

_____

_____

Complete Y
Meditation Y/N
32/56
Move on

Day 5 Health habit-breaker

Today we are going to practice what you learned at the start of the week by using **loving kindness** with a focus on health using a *digital detox.* Let's wake up to the idea that unplugging is a powerful way to restore balance and calm, which can only be a good thing for your health.

Commit today to disconnecting from the world when you finish your day's work. Use loving kindness by showing yourself self-compassion and a well-deserved break from constant connectivity. Now identify some positive intentions before you begin your digital detox – may this experience be great!

Record it below.

Day 5 Activity: Digital Detox

Duration: _____

Today's observations:

_____

_____

_____

_____

_____

_____

_____

_____

_____

_____

_____

Complete Y
Meditation Y/N
33/56
Move on

Day 6 Reflect & Recharge

This week, we focused on loving kindness as a means of developing compassion for ourselves and others. By becoming more self-compassionate, we open ourselves up to becoming more self-compassionate to others. We practised spending time in the green circle and discovering the joy of its soothing properties. We also focused on using loving kindness mediation as a means of developing the mind-body connection.

Please now complete the following:

Week 5 Reflections

What did you take away from this week's activities?

_____

_____

_____

_____

_____

_____

_____

_____

What are you grateful for?

_____

_____

_____

_____

_____

_____

_____

_____

_____

What were the 3 highlights of the week and which made you happy?

1._____

_____

_____

2._____

_____

_____

3._____

_____

_____

Complete Y
Meditation Y/N
34/56
Move on to Day 7

Day 7 Rest & Reward

Congratulations on making it to the end of the fifth week on the road to optimal well-being. Take time out today to rest. Before you move on to Week 6, please take the time to reward yourself with a treat. For example, a meal with friends, a small purchase, or simply by reminding yourself of the progress you have made.

Week 5 Reward: And Breathe....

My reward to myself for putting my well-being at the heart of what I do will be:

_____

_____

_____

_____

_____

_____

_____

Complete Y
35/56
Move on to Week 6

WEEK 6: THEME – FEEDING THE LOVE WOLF

Day 1 Insight

Day 2 Mind-body connector (free choice)

Day 3 Fitness habit-breaker (noticing the good)

Day 4 Nutrition habit-breaker (noticing the good)

Day 5 Health habit-breaker (noticing the good)

Day 6 Reflect & Recharge

Day 7 Rest & Reward

Day 1 Insight

"When your heart speaks take good notes."

—Judith Exner

Simply recognizing negative thoughts and that a problem exists is a good step toward solving it. Knowing that you have a negativity bias will help you to recognize when you're dwelling on the negative aspects of a situation due to this in-built bias we all possess. If you are constantly thinking about what you could have done (past thinking) and what you may do (future thinking), how is that going to help you live in the here and now (the present)?

Remember that our brains are like Velcro for negative experiences and like Teflon for positive ones. Therefore, when something positive happens to you, make it a point to take a moment to savour the experience and take in the good. Replay it in your mind a few times so the memory of the positive experience gets archived in your long-term memory.

Scheduling lots of fun moments throughout your week is a great way to start noticing the good and reaping the benefits. For example, have a cup of coffee outside in the mornings; take fifteen minutes a day to read something you find entertaining; buy fresh flowers for the house; use an essential oils diffuser to bring calming scents into your office; and spend some time out of the office each day. These small doses of positivity throughout the day will help your brain counteract its natural negativity. Whenever something negative happens to you—for example, someone says something mean to you, quickly follow this up with a thought or a memory that makes you happy or that you are grateful for. This is why we have recorded the 3 main highlights of our week every week in this book– we are learning to notice and take in the good. We are gradually rewiring your brain for happiness.

Habit-breaker exercise

Rick Hanson, the psychologist, says we have two wolves in our heart: one of hate and one of love. By taking in the good, we feed the love wolf and prevent our wolf of hate from taking over. This exercise comes from his book, *Just One Thing*. It has three parts. Today, aim to:

1. Notice a positive experience

This will probably be something quite normal, such as someone smiling at you as they walk past you, someone helping you with a task, the sun shining on your face as you walk to work, a memory of something good that happened to you, or someone showing you their appreciation by thanking you. Most positive experiences are quite ordinary and relatively minor— hence why we often ignore them and they go unnoticed. But they are still real and important for our psyche!

Now, whether it's something happening in the here or now or a memory, allow yourself to feel the pleasure of it. Let yourself *feel* good about it. Let it fully sink in.

Notice any hesitation you might feel to doing this and avoid thinking that if you allowed yourself to enjoy the pleasure of these small things, you'd somehow let your guard down and allow bad things to happen.

2. Stay with the experience

Now aim to stay with the experience for twenty, even thirty seconds. Try and avoid getting overly distracted by something or someone else. If you do get distracted, simply return to the experience (using the bus stop technique if needed). Allow yourself to really enjoy it and savour the experience for as long as you can, taking in the good. The longer you attend to this and the more emotionally stimulating it is, the stronger the trace in your memory.

3. Absorb the experience

Now enable the experience to be truly felt and absorbed, and open yourself up to taking in the good. You do this simply by staying with the experience and allowing yourself to feel it.

It might help you to know that while this positive experience is held in awareness, its related neural pathways are busily firing and wiring together. Try to do this a number of times a day. It doesn't take long—twenty, or even thirty seconds each time.

You are not trying to cling on to positive experiences for dear life. That would cause tension and probably lead to disappointment. Actually, you are doing the opposite: by taking them in, you will feel better fed inside and less fragile or needy.

Day 1 Activity: Noticing the good

Today's observations:

_____

_____

_____

_____

_____

_____

_____

_____

_____

Complete Y
36/56
Move on

Day 2 Mind-body connector

This week, you can choose from any of the mind-body connector techniques you have learned and practice daily. You can choose from:

* The body scan
* 7/11 Breathing
* Mindful movement
* The 3-minute break
* Loving kindness meditation

Day 2 Activity: Free Choice

Mind-Body Connector:

_____

Today's observations:

_____

_____

_____

_____

Complete Y
37/56
Move on

NOW AIM TO PRACTICE ANY OF THE MIND-BODY CONNECTOR TECHNIQUES EVERY DAY FOR THE REST OF THE WEEK ALONGSIDE YOUR DAILY ACTIVITY.

Day 3 Fitness habit-breaker

When you embark on your exercise today and something positive happens to you, you should make it a point to take a moment to savour the experience and **take in the good**. Replay it in your mind a few times so the memory of the positive experience gets archived in your long-term memory.

Day 3 Activity: Take in the Good

Experience:

_____

_____

Today's observations:

_____

_____

_____

_____

_____

_____

Mind-body connector Y/N
Complete Y
38/56
Move on

Day 4 Nutrition habit-breaker

When you eat a meal today, aim to notice and take in the good, such as smell, taste, sense of fulfilment from what it does for your suppression of hunger. You should make it a point to take a moment to savour the experience and **take in the good**. Replay it in your mind a few times so the memory of the positive experience gets archived in your long-term memory.

Day 4 Activity: Nutrition-Take in the Good

Experience:

_____

_____

_____

Today's observations:

_____

_____

_____

_____

_____

_____

_____

Mind-body connector Y/N
Complete Y
39/56
Move on

Day 5 Health habit-breaker

As a means of developing loving kindness and **taking in the good**, which ultimately has huge impact on your health, I highly recommend a technique known as an "area of refuge" in your brain. That is, have a list of positive things ready—such as good memories, inspiring quotes, or lines from poems—that you can think of whenever you find your mind wandering to a negative memory.

This is something I recommend you do. I call it my "mind jar," which I visualise in a symbolic way. I've memorized a memory that I love involving time with my son, and whenever I catch myself thinking about something negative from the past, I start to recite the memory in my head. I also recite the Japanese proverb at the start of this book: "Fall seven times stand up eight." Both of these immediately take my focus off the negative, which results in an instantaneous mood boost.

Day 5 Activity: Take in the Good

Three things for my Mind Jar:

1._____

_____

2._____

_____

3._____

_____

Today's observations:

_____

_____

_____

_____

_____

_____

Mind-body connector Y/N
Complete Y
40/56
Move on

Day 6 Reflect & Recharge

This week we focused on taking in the good as a means of reducing our in-built negativity bias and then building on positive experiences. We practised using mind-body connectors to come back to the senses as a means of developing the mind-body connection.

Please now complete the following:

Week 6 Reflections

What did you take away from this week's activities?

_____

_____

_____

_____

_____

_____

_____

_____

_____

What are you grateful for?

_____

_____

_____

_____

_____

_____

What were the 3 highlights of the week and which made you happy?

1._____

_____

2._____

_____

3._____

_____

Complete Y
Mind-body connector Y/N
41/56
Move on to Day 7

Day 7 Rest & Reward

Congratulations on making it to the end of the sixth week on the road to optimal well-being. Take time out today to rest. Before you move on to Week 7, please take the time to reward yourself with a treat, like a meal with friends, a small purchase, or simply by reminding yourself of the progress you have made.

Week 6 Reward: And Breathe....

My reward to myself for putting my well-being at the heart of what I do will be:

_____

_____

_____

_____

_____

_____

Complete Y
42/56
Move on to Week 7

WEEK 7: THEME – FINDING FLOW

Day 1 Day 1 insight

Day 2 Mind-body connector (free choice)

Day 3 Fitness habit-breaker (healthy sustainer)

Day 4 Nutrition habit-breaker (healthy sustainer)

Day 5 Health habit-breaker (healthy sustainer)

Day 6 Reflect & Recharge

Day 7 Rest & Reward

Day 1 – Insight

"Happiness is where we find it, but rarely where we seek it."
—J. Petit Senn

A good way to think of the different aspects of your life is to think of it like a recipe for a cake: it is made up of ingredients, all with different properties and in different quantities. Get the mixture out of kilter and the cake won't rise. Likewise, get your life recipe out of balance and it can have devastating impact on your health. (Remember back to my mother of all meltdowns? Trust me, it happens!).

Think about a healthy "life recipe": If you had no restrictions and were to make the perfect choice with no consequence to you or others (such as guilt, failure, overindulgence, lack of confidence, or fear), how important would each potential "ingredient" (each area of life that will enrich and nourish resilience) be to you?

The right combination of life cake recipe can help to nurture and feed your sense of well-being, contentment, and happiness, because, with the right balance, you enter into a state that psychologists call flow. Mihaly Csikszentmihalyi, one of the founding figures of positive psychology, has studied this phenomenon in depth and describes flow as "feeling strong alert, in effortless control." Although the term was mainly related to individual tasks, I feel it's every bit as relevant and helpful with work-life balance.

It doesn't mean chasing happiness (we learned that earlier). It means feeling nourished and feeling what you do is worthwhile, connecting, and most of all that you love it for its own sake. If you have this, *flow* will emerge and from flow, happiness will come.

Habit-breaker exercise

So, if you had a nourishing life recipe, what would the ingredients of your life cake consist of? How important would you rate each of them—regardless of where you are now? (On a scale of 1-10, where 1 = "I am not at all bothered" and 10 = "this life ingredient would be extremely important"?)

If you could re-write the recipe and choose again, how would you rate your "Cake" life recipe? Using the following categories to rate where you are now and where you would like each one to be in the near future.

Health? Intimacy? Parenting? Family? Work? Friendship? Learning? Leisure? Spirituality? Community?

_____

_____

_____

_____

Ask yourself:

How close to your ideal "life cake" recipe have you been during the past few months, compared with where you want to be? Have you overindulged on one ingredient and neglected others? If so, what are they? In other words, how aware have you been of how important the various "ingredients" are and How much do you feel your current life cake recipe has been in line with what's most important to you?

As you notice the deficiencies, how does it make you feel? Use loving kindness to yourself with what shows up. You may not like what you have neglected, but stay with the unpleasantness of it. How might that inform a change of direction? What might that be?

I would ask yourself to consider whether you can afford to ignore what your body may be telling you. We like to ignore the cues—remember back to what my body was telling me? When I was burnt out, all the physical symptoms were there—headaches, tinnitus, exhaustion, lack of energy, to name a few—telling me to make the change.

The problem was the first things I dropped from my life were things not very essential, things that didn't entail letting others down very badly: going to the gym, seeing my friends, spending time with my husband, playing with my son. We all do it, but the problem here is that it's these very things that we enjoy, that nourish us, and that make us feel glad to be alive.

When we drop something from the green circle, we feel a little more stressed because we didn't do one of the things that helps to keep us nourished, while at the same time we do continue doing all those things that deplete us and make us feel even more stressed. So we feel something else is going to have to go next time. What? Something else we enjoy and that won't let others down very much. As a result, by the end of the process, we feel even more depleted—so something else has got to go…

You can see where this is going. It's a vicious circle that sinks you further into the pit of despair than you were when you started out!

The final destination for a life that has been out of balance for a sustained period of time is likely to be exhaustion, stress, and unhappiness. It's like a funnel that, when you engage in a full life with work, family, friends, hobbies, interests, etc., you experience true well-being. When life has been stripped back to merely doing those things we have to do to keep alive—work, cleaning, food shopping, etc., our well-being invariably suffers.

A good way to sum this up is that a healthy mind is a healthy body and a healthy body is a healthy mind. It's all interrelated.

Habit-breaker exercise

Take some time to think about all the things that sustain you—activities that you enjoy and that are life-enhancing. Write them down in the left hand column below. Now consider all the things in your life that tend to drain your energy, that you don't enjoy and that deplete your energy. Write them down in the right hand column.

Sustainers	Drainers
_____	_____
_____	_____
_____	_____
_____	_____
_____	_____
_____	_____
_____	_____
_____	_____
_____	_____
_____	_____

Are there ways in which you can reduce the drainers and increase the sustainers in your life?

This week, we are going to ask you to spend time taking in the good and feeding the love wolf by picking a sustainer and engaging in it. We will also aim to reduce drainers from our lives.

Day 1 Activity: A Healthy Sustainer

What to keep:

_____

_____

_____

_____

_____

What to lose:

_____

_____

_____

_____

_____

Today's observations:

_____

_____

_____

_____

_____

_____

_____

_____

Complete Y

43/56

Move on

 Day 2 Mind-body connector

This week you can choose from any of the mind-body connector techniques you have learned and practice daily. You can choose from:

* The body scan
* 7/11 Breathing
* Mindful movement
* The 3-minute break
* Loving kindness meditation

Day 2 Activity: Free Choice

Mind-Body Connector:

_____

Today's observations:

_____

_____

_____

_____

_____

_____

_____

_____

_____

Complete Y
44/56
Move on

NOW AIM TO PRACTICE ANY OF THE MIND-BODY CONNECTOR TECHNIQUES EVERY DAY ALONGSIDE YOUR DAILY ACTIVITY.

Day 3 Fitness habit-breaker

Today we are going to practice what you learnt at the start of the week by using the **life-sustainer** model with a *focus on fitness*. Consider all the things you want to keep that help you to maintain your exercise regime, and then consider all the things that act as drainers.

Now write down the number-one thing you will keep and the number one thing you will lose in order to help you progress with your fitness.

Day 3 Activity: Fitness-Healthy Sustainer

Sustainer to practice:

_____

_____

Drainer I will lose:

_____

_____

Today's observations:

_____

_____

_____

_____

_____

_____

_____

_____

_____

_____

_____

_____

Mind-body connector Y/N
Complete Y
45/56
Move on

Day 4 Nutrition habit-breaker

Today we are going to practice what you learned at the start of the week by using the **life-sustainer** model with a *focus on nutrition*. Consider all the things you want to keep that help you to maintain your diet and balanced eating regime and then consider all the things that act as drainers.

Now write down the number one thing you will keep and the number one thing you will lose to help you progress with your nutrition.

Day 4 Activity: Nutrition-Healthy Sustainer

Sustainer to practice:

_____

_____

Drainer I will lose:

_____

_____

Today's observations:

_____

_____

_____

_____

_____

_____

_____

_____

Mind-body connector Y/N
Complete Y
46/56
Move on

Day 5 Health habit-breaker

Today we are going to practice what you learned at the start of the week by using the **life-sustainer** model with a *focus on health*. Make a list of the six people who make you feel happiest in your life and photograph this onto your phone. Remember: happiness makes you healthy!

Whenever you feel stress building, pick up your phone and call one. Take in the good, and let this be a great life sustainer for you.

Day 5 Activity: Healthy Sustainer

1. _____

2. _____

3. _____

4. _____

5. _____

6. _____

Today's observations:

_____

_____

_____

_____

_____

_____

_____

_____

_____

_____

Mind-body connector Y/N
Complete Y
47/56
Move on

Day 6 Reflect & Recharge

This week we focused on healthy sustainers and drainers as a means of understanding what your ideal "life cake" recipe is and what you need to do to improve the recipe on all four pillars of health. We practised using mind-body connectors as a means of developing the mind-body connection.

Please now complete the following:

Week 7 Reflections

What did you take away from this week's activities?

_____

_____

_____

_____

_____

_____

_____

_____

_____

What are you grateful for?

_____

_____

_____

_____

_____

What were the 3 highlights of the week and which made you happy?

1._____

_____

_____

2._____

_____

_____

3._____

_____

_____

Complete Y
Mind-body connector Y/N
48/56
Move on to Day 7

Day 7 Rest & Reward

Congratulations on making it to the end of the seventh week on the road to optimal well-being. Take time out today to rest. Remember: we all need to slow down in order to speed up.

Before you move on to Week 8, please take the time to reward yourself with a treat, such as a meal with friends, a small purchase, or simply by reminding yourself of the progress you have made.

Week 7 Reward: And Breathe....

My reward to myself for putting my well-being at the heart of what I do will be:

_____

_____

_____

_____

_____

_____

_____

_____

Complete Y
49/56
Move on to Week 8

WEEK 8: THEME – NOURISHING RESILIENCE

Day 1 Insight

Day 2 Mind-body connector (free choice)

Day 3 Fitness habit-breaker (nourishing resilience)

Day 4 Nutrition habit-breaker (nourishing resilience)

Day 5 Health habit-breaker (nourishing resilience)

Day 6 Reflect & Recharge

Day 7 Rest & Reward

Day 1 Insight

"I am not what happened to me, I am what I choose to become."
—Carl Gustav Jung

Nourishing resilience is about pulling all you have learned together to enable you to bring mindfulness into your everyday life and maintain a mindful approach to your well-being. The greater your well-being, the greater your resilience and vice versa.

Over the course of the last eight weeks, you have learned to:

- ➤ Wake up and notice
- ➤ Come to your senses
- ➤ Engage in mindfulness of thought
- ➤ Embrace difficulty
- ➤ Spend time in the green circle
- ➤ Feed the love wolf
- ➤ Find flow
- ➤ Nourish resilience

I hope you will continue to practice the mindfulness techniques above and incorporate them into your daily well-being regime where appropriate. They can also be used for general life and can easily be integrated into your daily activities.

I do hope you also continue to practice the mind-body connectors you learned (body scan, 7/11 breathing, mindful movement, the 3-minute break, and loving kindness meditation). I outline below easy ways to sprinkle them into your day.

My top tips for a mindful day are:

Morning mindfulness

I recommend, whenever possible, you start the day with a body scan and mindful breathing. An easy time to do this is when you first wake up and whilst you are lying in bed. Set your alarm clock ten minutes earlier to allow you to have a mindful start to your day.

One task we all do before we start our day is brush our teeth. Use this opportunity as one small thing you can do where you tune in to noticing and coming to the senses whilst completing a task that, more often than not, we do on automatic pilot.

Lunchtime Mindfulness

The one really simple request I ask you to do each and every day is *to take a break*. Aim to get double benefit by trying to make this a green break: the ideal break is outside, amongst nature.

Afternoon Mindfulness

Before you end your working day, aim to take in the good. Whether that means acknowledging what you are grateful for or telling someone something you appreciated as a means of embracing a good experience, take in the good and feed the love wolf! Remember to hold onto the experience for about twenty seconds.

Evening Mindfulness

Aim to spend some time in the green circle every evening. Not only will doing something soothing allow you to build positive emotions, but it will also relax and calm the body before bed. Whether that is watching a movie, reading a book, or spending time with family, do something that soothes you and that you enjoy.

Bedtime Mindfulness

Switch off your phone at least one hour before you go to bed, and disconnect from being in "doing" mode. It's the best prep for a good night's sleep you could do. Engage in the body scan or 7/11 breathing technique to help relax you fully before sleep. Consider investing in a mindfulness app to access sleep meditations (you can get this on the Soulgenic app).

Habit-breaker Exercise

Aim to practice the above by engaging in a mindful day. Describe it in the space below.

Day 1 Activity: A Mindful Day

Today's observations:

_____

_____

_____

_____

_____

_____

_____

_____

Complete Y
50/56
Move on

 ## Day 2 Mind-body connector

This week you can choose from any of the mind-body connector techniques you have learned and practice daily. You can choose from:

* The body scan
* 7/11 Breathing
* Mindful movement
* The 3-minute break
* Loving kindness meditation

Day 2 Activity: Free Choice

Mind-Body Connector:

_____

Today's observations:

_____

_____

_____

_____

_____

_____

_____

_____

_____

_____

Complete Y

51/56

Move on

NOW AIM TO PRACTICE ANY OF THE MIND-BODY CONNECTOR TECHNIQUES EVERY DAY ALONGSIDE YOUR DAILY ACTIVITY.

Day 3 Fitness habit-breaker

Using all you have learned over the last few weeks, aim to do a mindful exercise session (minimum thirty minutes of exercise) to include the following focus:

- ✓ Warm up – mindful breathing
- ✓ Main – mindful movement and body scan
- ✓ Cool down – mindful breathing and taking in the good
- ✓ Post workout – the green circle - sauna or steam or equivalent

Day 3 Activity: Fitness – Nourishing Resistance

Exercise session:

_____

_____

_____

_____

_____

_____

_____

_____

Today's observations:

_____

_____

_____

_____

_____

_____

_____

_____

Complete Y
Mind-body connector Y/N
52/56
Move on

Day 4 Nutrition habit-breaker

Using all you have learned over the last few weeks, aim to do a mindful nutrition session (cooking a two-course meal from scratch) to include the following focus:

- ✓ Buying meal ingredients – loving kindness
- ✓ Setting the table – loving kindness
- ✓ Meal prep – taking in the good
- ✓ Meal time – noticing one small thing, breathing & taking in the good

Day 4 Activity: Nutrition – Nourishing Resistance

Meal choice:

_____

_____

_____

_____

_____

Today's observations:

_____

_____

_____

_____

_____

_____

_____

Complete Y
Mind-body connector Y/N
53/56
Move on

Day 5 Health habit-breaker

Using all you have learned over the last few weeks, aim to do a mindful health session by reading a book. Aim to come to your senses; use mindfulness of thought and the bus stop when you get distracted. Take in the good with the joy of spending some time in the green circle.

Day 5 Activity: Health – Nourishing Resistance

Book choice:

_____

Today's observations:

_____

_____

_____

_____

_____

_____

Complete Y
Mind-body connector Y/N
54/56
Move on

Day 6 Reflect & Recharge

This week we focused on pulling all you have learned together with a view to practicing the mindful day! We also practiced using a range of mindfulness techniques on all four pillars of health. The mind-body connectors were also practiced as a means of developing the mind-body connection.

Please now complete the following:

Week 8 Reflections

What did you take away from this week's activities?

_____

_____

_____

_____

_____

_____

_____

_____

_____

_____

What are you grateful for?

_____

_____

_____

_____

_____

_____

_____

What were the highlights of the 8 weeks, and which made you happy?

_____

_____

_____

_____

_____

_____

_____

_____

_____

_____

_____

What are the key takeaways you will pledge to carry on with as you complete this journey?

_____

_____

_____

_____

_____

_____

_____

_____

_____

_____

_____

_____

_____

Complete Y
Mind-body connector Y/N
55/56
Move on to Day 7

Day 7 Rest & Reward

Congratulations on making it to the end of the eight weeks on your road to optimal well-being. Take time out today to celebrate what you have achieved and just how far you have come.

Week 8 Reward: And Breathe....

My reward to myself for putting my well-being at the heart of what I do will be:

_____

_____

_____

_____

_____

_____

_____

Complete Y
56/56

BIG CONGRATULATIONS – YOU HAVE COMPLETED THE EIGHT WEEK COURSE!!!

Chapter 5

Moving Forward

WHERE ARE YOU NOW?

Take time to look back and consider what you wanted to achieve in terms of your well-being and compare it to where you are now. After careful consideration and reflection complete the sections below:

By the end of the 8 weeks, I wanted to achieve:

_____

_____

_____

_____

_____

_____

_____

I am here now and I achieved...?

_____

_____

_____

_____

_____

_____

_____

_____

_____

_____

_____

_____

_____

_____

_____

Did you achieve what you set out to achieve? Y/N

Do you still suffer stress on a regular basis? Y/N

Do you now eat mindfully? Y/N

Do you now take exercise mindfully? Y/N

Do you now feel a mind-body connection? Y/N

Is there anything else hindering your health? Y/N

Write down your biggest achievement from completing this book:

_____

_____

_____

_____

_____

_____

_____

_____

Commit to doing one small thing to continue to improve...

Your well-being:

_____

_____

Your fitness:

_____

_____

Your nutrition:

_____

_____

Your mind-body:

_____

_____

Your health:

_____

_____

The reward I promised myself was:

_____

_____

You have given yourself the reward of....?

_____

_____

_____

_____

_____

_____

_____

###

Final Advice

AS WE FINISH this journey together, here is my final advice to you:

- ❖ Continue to *invest in your continued education* – read, gain a mentor, keep an open mind.

- ❖ Invest in your *ongoing well-being* – nutrition, exercise, mindfulness, and health. Eight weeks of mindfulness is proven to change the grey matter of the brain, eliminating unhealthy negative schemas and behaviour patterns that may limit your success. You have completed the hardest part, so please keep it going and reap the benefits.

- ❖ *Accept compliments.* Take responsibility for your success, and set your sails of thought for altitudes of achievement which stagger the imagination.

❖ *Change your mantra.* You have to use your password throughout the day for computer access so set this as a mantra for optimal living. Use it as a modern-day pledge to how you want to live your live and let it act as a mindful daily reminder for a healthy life. This could be:

- BUILDNEW@LIFE
- EATCLEAN@HEART
- BEHXXPY@HOME
- FITNESSFOR@FUN
- MINDFULNESSFOR@WELL-BEING

I leave you with a poem that works for me:

If you think you are beaten, you are
If you think you dare not, you don't
If you like to win, but you think you can't
It's almost certain you won't.
If you think you'll lose, you're lost
For out of the world we find,
Success begins with a fellow's will
It's all in the state of mind.

If you think you are outclassed, you are.

You have got to think high to rise

You've got to be sure of yourself before

You can ever win a prize.

Life's battles don't always go to the stronger or faster man

But sooner or later the man who wins is the man WHO THINKS HE CAN!

—Napoleon Hill, *Think and Grow Rich*

###

My Gift to You!

I AM FOREVER grateful that you chose to read my book. I want to give you a gift!

I am offering you the chance to continue on a wellness journey with me by using my four-pillar approach through my very own Soulgenic online app. Here are five reasons why Soulgenic will help you to achieve your goals:

1. Suitable for all: Like this book, Soulgenic's approach to wellness is perfectly balanced, covering fitness, nutrition, mind-body, and health.

2. An easy-to-follow programme: You'll enjoy a series of 28-day programmes of fun and challenging video sessions delivered to you daily, to stay on track

3. Part of your daily routine: Our activities can all be done in less than thirty minutes, ensuring health and fitness become part of your daily routine.

4. Earn rewards as you progress: With Soulgenic, your wellness is rewarded. Earn points and rewards for being active. The more you do, the more you are rewarded.

5. Support & motivation: Soulgenic is always there for you, giving you the motivation and support you need to succeed every day.

Go to book.clubsoulgenic.co.uk and register to receive 20% off your very own wellness journey, where you can continue to implement a four-pillar approach to your well-being.

If you want to contact me, email glenda@soulgenic.com.

I would love to hear from you and encourage you to share your stories with me about how the techniques in this book and my online programme have helped you achieve sustainable lifelong wellness.

I am confident this book will reward you with healthy life-changing habits, and the online programme will continue to offer you ongoing support.

THANK YOU FROM THE BOTTOM OF MY HEART

Acknowledgements

I WAS LUCKY ENOUGH to have a chance meeting with Dr. Alessio Agostinis, from which my love for mindfulness was born. It has been a privilege to work with Alessio and have him as a guide through the mindfulness arena. Alessio and I subsequently developed an 8-week mindfulness for well-being course for entrepreneurs, based on the central tenants of MBSR and the UK Breathworks package, and I use some of these techniques within the book. I have grown immeasurably by being introduced to mindfulness, and I continue to reap the benefits daily in my own practice.

I want to thank my colleagues in fitness training (Kenny Manson), nutrition (Kit Chamier), health (Dr Andrew Mitchell), and mind-body disciplines (Daniel Ireland). They have been a source of inspiration and feedback in the writing of this book's content.

My deepest gratitude goes to AJ Mihrzad and Pat Pilla for their ongoing unwavering support and expertise in helping me to bring this book to fruition. Big thanks also to the other writers I shared time with at AJ's book retreat—without them I wouldn't have developed the creativity whilst gaining vital feedback as I progressed my ideas.

While this book is of considerable significance to me, I do hope that people from all walks of life may find something of significance for them within the fold of its covers.

About the Author

DR. GLENDA RIVOALLAN describes herself as an entrepreneur, wellness expert, and learning junkie who is extremely passionate about helping the maximum number of people live healthier lives. She has spent the last twenty-four years in the wellness industry, studying exercise behaviour and trends, and is steadfast in her belief that we should all be able to achieve a happy life through a commitment to our holistic well-being. Glenda learned to appreciate the irony that her life as an entrepreneur has, at times, made her well-being suffer.

Glenda had a major turning point in her life when she stumbled upon the practice of mindfulness. Through an ongoing commitment to the techniques she learned, she developed a newfound appreciation for mindful exercise, mindful nutrition, mindful health, and the all-important mind-body connection.

As CEO and founder of Soulgenic, Glenda's vision is take her unique Soulgenic wellness journey to the masses and reward people for their wellness through technology that is integrated with their existing way of life. The creation of Club Soulgenic, a fully integrated well-being and fitness club, is a fitting testament to the home of the brand and is synonymous with the values of Soulgenic online product.

Prior to Soulgenic, Glenda was founder and director of the multiple-award-winning health club brand Healthhaus. She has over 200 club openings under her belt, so it's safe to say she knows her way around a gym.

Glenda was born in Scotland and is now based in a small island called Jersey in the Channel Islands near France. She is married to Jean, has a son called Kaden and a dog called Marley. She loves nothing more than walking the dog with her family on one of Jersey's beautiful beaches, which she says is a mindful act all of its own.

Glenda is a straight-talking businesswoman who is a regular guest speaker on radio and at conferences on all things well-being. Her personal interest in the factors that lead to entrepreneurial success resulted in her studying the role of mindfulness in developing resilience in entrepreneurs. She will complete her Doctorate in Business Administration (DBA) this summer.

Glenda's favorite quote sums up her love for entrepreneurship. It comes from Drucker, who says: "The best way to predict the future is to create it."

And her take on the value of wellness is this: "Well, simply put, no one ever died from being too healthy!"

###

Printed in Great Britain
by Amazon